THE CHRONICLES OF

CONAN

VOLUME 9

RIDERS OF THE RIVER-DRAGONS
AND OTHER STORIES

THE CHRONICLES OF

CONAN®

VOLUME 9

RIDERS OF THE RIVER-DRAGONS
AND OTHER STORIES

based on the classic pulp
character Conan the Barbarian,
created by

ROBERT E. HOWARD

written by

ROY THOMAS

illustrated by

JOHN BUSCEMA, VAL MAYERIK,
and others

coloring by

PETER DAWES, WIL GLASS,
IAN SOKOLIWSKI, and DONOVAN YACIUK
with ALL THUMBS CREATIVE

DARK HORSE BOOKS™

publisher
MIKE RICHARDSON

collection designer
M. JOSHUA ELLIOTT

art director
LIA RIBACCHI

collection editor
JEREMY BARLOW

Special thanks to Fredrik Malmberg and Thommy Wojciechowski at
Conan Properties, Arthur Lieberman at Lieberman & Norwalk, LLP,
Marco Lupoi at Panini, Scott Allie, Kurt Busiek, Lance Kreiter,
and Roy Thomas.

This volume collects issues sixty through sixty-three, sixty-five, and sixty-nine through
seventy-one of the Marvel comic-book series **Conan the Barbarian**.

Published by Dark Horse Books
A division of Dark Horse Comics, Inc.
10956 SE Main Street
Milwaukie, OR 97222

www.darkhorse.com
www.conan.com

To find a comics shop in your area, call the Comic Shop Locator Service
toll-free at 1-888-266-4226

First edition November 2005
ISBN: 1-59307-394-1

1 3 5 7 9 10 8 6 4 2

Printed in China

TABLE OF CONTENTS

ALL STORIES WRITTEN BY ROY THOMAS

"Know, O prince, that between the years when the oceans drank Atlantis and the gleaming cities, and the rise of the sons of Aryas, there was an Age undreamed of, when shining kingdoms lay spread across the world like blue mantles beneath the stars.

"Hither came Conan, the Cimmerian, black-haired, sullen-eyed, sword in hand, a thief, a reaver, a slayer, with gigantic melancholies and gigantic mirth, to tread the jeweled thrones of the Earth under his sandaled feet."

—The Nemedian Chronicles.

WELL, CONAN? DO YOU-- *YIELD?*

YOU'RE *STRONG,* AYE--

BUT, WILL YOU NOW *ADMIT--* THAT AT LEAST *TWO* OF US-- CAN *BEST* YOU?

ON THE DAY-- THAT YOU *CAN,* M'GORA...

...YOU'LL BE THE *FIRST* TO KNOW OF IT...

...BUT, THIS IS *NOT* THAT DAY!

¡UHNNN--!

DAGON'S EYE!

YOU-- MAKE US ALL-- FEEL *SHAMED,* CIMMERIAN.

FOR THREE YEARS, WE CORSAIRS HAVE RAVAGED THE COASTS OF *KUSH* AND POINTS NORTH...

YET, *YOU* CAN DEFEAT ANY *TWO* OF US!

CAST OFF THOSE FEELINGS OF SHAME, M'GORA.

THAT'S NOT WHY I CHALLENGED YOU AND YASUNGA TO *GRAPPLE* WITH ME.

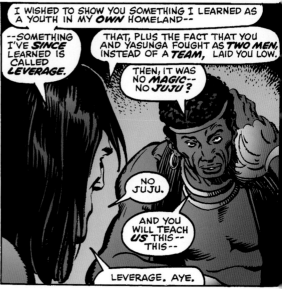

I WISHED TO SHOW YOU SOMETHING I LEARNED AS A YOUTH IN MY *OWN* HOMELAND--

--SOMETHING I'VE *SINCE* LEARNED IS CALLED *LEVERAGE.*

THAT, PLUS THE FACT THAT YOU AND YASUNGA FOUGHT AS *TWO MEN,* INSTEAD OF A *TEAM,* LAID YOU LOW.

THEN, IT WAS NO *MAGIC--* NO *JUJU?*

NO JUJU.

AND YOU WILL TEACH *US* THIS-- THIS--

LEVERAGE. AYE.

8

BUT MEANWHILE, WE'VE STILL SEEN NO *HYBORIAN SHIPS* LATELY-- AND WE COULD ALL USE SOME *EXERCISE.*

LARANGA! AJONGA! JOIN M'GORA, AND SEE IF *THREE* OF YOU CAN BEST A POOR, TIRED OLD *CIMMERIAN!*

AS YOU *WISH,* CONAN...

CROM KNOWS, YOUR *FELLOWS* WILL CHEER YOU ON LOUDLY ENOUGH.

BUT, YOU MUST KNOW IT IS ONLY *NATURAL* FOR US CORSAIRS TO WANT ONE OF OUR *OWN* TO WIN--

--RATHER THAN A *WHITE-SKIN* WHO JOINED US ONLY A *SHORT TIME* AGO.

MY *SKIN* IS WHITE-- BUT SWEAT AND BLOOD ARE THE SAME COLOR FOR *ALL* MEN, M'GORA.

NOW, *HAVE AT YOU*--

AYE, AND SEE IF YOU CAN WASTE ANY *MORE* OF MY PRECIOUS TIME!

BÊLIT!

I *FEAR,* CONAN, THAT OUR WRESTLING BOUT IS *FINISHED.*

YOU'RE A *HARD CAPTAIN,* BÊLIT...

...DENYING YOUR MEN A BIT OF *SPORT.*

WHAT SPORT? YOU'LL *BRAWL* ALL DAY, AND *DRINK* ALL NIGHT...

...WHILE THE *STYGIANS* AND THEIR ILK RAKE IN ALL THE *GOLD!*

BE *FAIR,* WOMAN!

YOU KNOW WE'VE *FRIGHTENED OFF* MOST SHIPPING FROM THESE LANES.

SO YOU SQUABBLE AMONG *YOURSELVES* TO PROVE YOU'RE *REAL MEN!*

WELL, THERE ARE *OTHER* WAYS OF FIGHTING THAN WITH SWEAT AND *SINEW.*

YOU AND I, MY LOVER, HAVE NEVER *CROSSED SWORDS.*

PERHAPS IT'S TIME WE *DID* SO...

...ALL IN THE INTERESTS OF *EXERCISE,* AS YOU PUT IT.

LARANGA-- MY *BLADE!*

AND *MINE,* YASUNGA.

STILL, GIRL, *YOU* WERE RAISED AMONG THESE *BLACKS,* WHO FIGHT MOSTLY WITH *ARROW* AND *SPEAR.*

IT'S *NO FEAT* FOR ME TO BEST YOU WITH A *SWORD.*

NO FEAT, IS IT?

WHY, YOU CONCEITED, ARROGANT, OVER-MUSCLED--!

THE PIRATE QUEEN'S NEXT PHRASE IS MERCIFULLY COVERED OVER BY THE LUSTY CLANG OF MEETING BLADES...

THEN, WITH A SPEED THAT BELIES HIS MORE THAN TWO HUNDRED POUNDS, THE BRAWNY BARBARIAN SIDESTEPS HIS CAPTAIN'S OVER-HASTY LUNGE...

...ONLY TO SEE THE FLAMES OF FURY GROW IN THOSE DARKSOME EYES...

...MOMENT BY MOMENT... THRUST BY ANGRY THRUST...

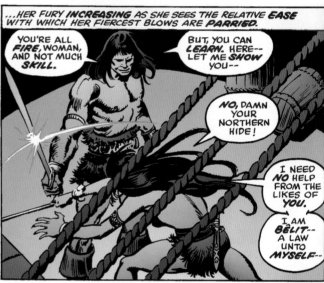

...HER FURY INCREASING AS SHE SEES THE RELATIVE EASE WITH WHICH HER FIERCEST BLOWS ARE PARRIED.

YOU'RE ALL FIRE, WOMAN, AND NOT MUCH SKILL.

BUT, YOU CAN LEARN. HERE-- LET ME SHOW YOU--

NO, DAMN YOUR NORTHERN HIDE!

I NEED NO HELP FROM THE LIKES OF YOU.

I AM BÊLIT-- A LAW UNTO MYSELF--

I AM BÊLIT!

AT THE LAST INSTANT, CONAN MOVES HIS HEAD-- AVOIDING A SLICE THAT WOULD HAVE SPLIT HIS SKULL LIKE A RIPE WARM MELON!

BY CROM, GIRL-- I LOVE YOU, AND ALL THAT--

--BUT THIS HAS GONE FAR ENOUGH!

THAT VISELIKE GRIP HAS HELD THE STRONG-EST MEN MOTIONLESS.

AGAINST IT, NO WOMAN-- NOT EVEN BÊLIT-- CAN HOPE TO PREVAIL.

THEN, *FIRES OF MADNESS* DIE IN DARK EYES AS QUICKLY AS THEY WERE BORN...

CONAN! OH, MY *CONAN*-- WHAT WAS I *DOING*??

IF I'D *SLAIN* YOU, IN THE *HEAT OF ANGER*--!

YOU'RE A *FIERCE* WARRIOR, *BÊLIT*... ONE OF THE *FIERCEST*.

IT IS *HARD* FOR ME TO ACCEPT ANY *LIMITS* WHEN IT COMES TO *FIGHTING*, CONAN.

TELL ME-- WAS THERE *EVER* A WOMAN YOU KNEW WHO COULD COMPARE WITH THE *BEST OF MEN* IN SWORDPLAY?

WELLLLL... THERE WAS *ONE*.

RED SON-YA WAS HER NAME-- THOUGH I MYSELF NEVER CROSSED SWORDS WITH HER.

BUT, THE DAY YOU CAN GET THRU *MY* GUARD WITH A SWORD, I *DESERVE* TO DIE.

SHE'D VOWED NEVER TO *LOVE* A MAN-- EXCEPT ONE WHO HAD *DEFEATED* HER IN BATTLE.

CROM TAKE ME, BUT IT MIGHT JUST HAVE BEEN WORTH THE *RISK!*

SO-- YOU THINK OF *OTHER WOMEN* WHILE YOU PAW OVER *ME*, DO YOU? I'LL--

WHOA, GIRL-- *WHOA!*

SON-YA AND I WERE BUT *FRIENDS*, AND NOT ALWAYS *THAT*...

...WHILE *YOU AND I*, THOUGH WE MET FIRST AS *FOES*-- AND THOUGH I BECAME YOUR SECOND-IN-COMMAND MOSTLY TO ESCAPE *WALKING THE PLANK*...

...YOU AND I ARE FAR *MORE* THAN FRIENDS!

ARE WE, CONAN?

ARE WE?

WOMEN! I'LL *NEVER* FATHOM YOU!

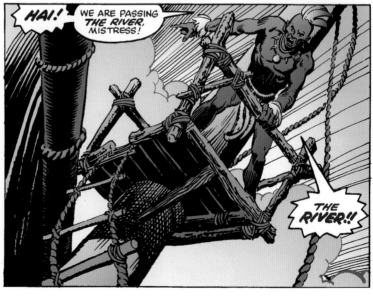

HAI! WE ARE PASSING *THE RIVER*, MISTRESS!

THE RIVER!!

11

LOOK AT IT, CIMMERIAN!

THERE AT YONDER SHORE IS THE RIVER *ZARKHEBA*, WHICH IS *DEATH!*

ITS WATERS ARE *POISONOUS*-- AND NOT EVEN CROCODILES, BUT ONLY *VENOMOUS* REPTILES, CAN LIVE IN IT.

THE BLACK PEOPLE *SHUN* IT-- AND *CRY OUT* TO EACH OTHER WHEN THEY EVEN *SEE* ITS GAPING, LIFELESS *MOUTH!*

SOUNDS LIKE A PLACE WORTH *AVOIDING*...

BUT, YOU SOUND AS IF YOU KNOW *MORE* OF IT THAN YOU'VE *SAID*.

SO I *DO*... AND I'LL *TELL* YOU THAT MORE, SOME DAY WHEN IT'S *TIME*.

TODAY-- WE SAIL ON *SOUTH!*

AND WHAT *BETTER* DIRECTION FOR THE TIGRESS TO SAIL --GIVING THE NORTHERN LANDS TIME TO *RE-BUILD* THEIR LUCRATIVE SHIPPING TRADE, *FREE* FROM FEARS OF THE *BLACK CORSAIRS*--

--THE BETTER FOR *BÊLIT* AND CREW TO HEAD NORTH AND *RAID* AGAIN, AT A LATER DATE !

AS FOR *CONAN*, HE LITTLE CARES *WHERE* THEY SAIL. *BÊLIT'S* IS THE MIND THAT DIRECTS THEIR RAIDS-- *HIS* THE ARM THAT CARRIES THEM OUT.

HE CARES ONLY THAT THEY *SAIL* AND *FIGHT*; HE FINDS THE LIFE *GOOD.*

AT LENGTH, DAYS LATER, A *SECOND* LARGE RIVER IS SIGHTED-- FAR *SOUTH* NOW OF KUSH--

THERE IS THE PLACE WE SEEK...

...THAT MORE *PEACEABLE* RIVER.

THE *WATAMBI TRIBE* THAT DWELLS AT ITS MOUTH OFFERS ME *TRIBUTE*, IN THE FORM OF *IVORY*, WHENEVER THE *TIGRESS* PASSES THIS WAY...

...AND I GIVE *THEM* A GIFT, IN *TURN*.

WHAT GIFT IS *THAT?*

WHY, WHAT *ELSE*, MY BARBARIAN-- BUT THE GOLDEN GIFT OF *LIFE*--

--TILL *NEXT* I COME AROUND!

CROM KNOWS, I'M NOT *SQUEAMISH* ABOUT USING *FORCE*, WOMAN--

BUT, DON'T YOU THINK YOU MIGHT *TRADE*, INSTEAD, SOME OF THE *LESSER* THINGS WE'VE LOOTED FROM THE *WHITE* LANDS-- AND GET EVEN *MORE* IVORY?

TUSKS WERE AT A *PREMIUM*, WHEN I FLED *ARGOS*.

I'LL *CONSIDER* THAT LINE OF REASONING... *NEXT* TRIP.

RIGHT *NOW*, HOWEVER...

HO, OMBASSA!

I KNOW YOU'RE *IN* THERE!

IT IS *BÊLIT* WHO CALLS YOU FORTH!

WE KNOW *FULL WELL* WHO CALLS, GODDESS.

WE *HIDE OUR HEADS* IN SHAME BECAUSE, THIS TIME-- WE'VE *NO IVORY* FOR YOU.

NO IVORY!?

WHY, YOU *DIRTY, THIEVING*--!

STAY YOUR HAND, WOMAN! IT'S *OBVIOUS* HE AND HIS TRIBESMEN DON'T WANT YOUR CORSAIRS *LEVELLING* THEIR VILLAGE.

SO WHY NOT LISTEN TO WHAT HE HAS TO *SAY*?

YOU ARE *WISE*, WHITE-SKIN... *WHOEVER* YOU BE.

WE *KNEW* IT WAS THE SEASON FOR YOU TO PAY US YOUR *VISIT*, GODDESS... AND WE HAD *IVORY IN PLENTY* FOR YOU.

BUT THE *RIDERS* TOOK IT-- *THE RIDERS OF THE RIVER-DRAGONS!*

RIDERS OF THE *WHAT*?

I'VE HEARD *TALL TALES* OF THEM-- MEN WHO RIDE *STANDING*, THEY SAY, UPON THE BACKS OF HUGE *CROCODILES*.

BUT, I'VE NEVER HEARD THE LEGEND USED TO KEEP ME FROM MY RIGHTFUL *TRIBUTE*.

THIS IS *NO* LEGEND, GODDESS.

I *BEG* YOU-- COME BACK WITH US TO OUR *VILLAGE*--

13

FOR, TONIGHT WE DO *GREAT JUJU* TO WARD OFF THE RIDERS-OF-DRAGONS FROM COMING *AGAIN*...

AND *YOUR PRESENCE* WILL ADD TO OUR *MAGIC!*

WE'LL COME-- BUT ONLY TO DECIDE IF YOU SPEAK THE *TRUTH.*

M'GORA-- TAKE *HALF* OUR MEN BACK TO THE *TIGRESS!*

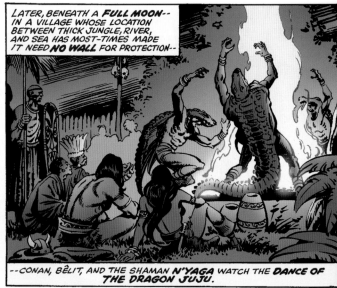

LATER, BENEATH A *FULL MOON*-- IN A VILLAGE WHOSE LOCATION BETWEEN THICK JUNGLE, RIVER, AND SEA HAS MOST-TIMES MADE IT NEED *NO WALL* FOR PROTECTION--

--CONAN, BÊLIT, AND THE SHAMAN N'YAGA WATCH THE *DANCE OF THE DRAGON JUJU.*

I WORSHIP *CIVILIZED* GODS, LIKE ISHTAR AND ASHTORETH.

I DON'T LIKE THIS *MUMMERY*-- THIS DANCING IN *REPTILE-SKINS.*

WHY DO THEY DRESS UP LIKE THE THINGS THEY *HATE,* SHAMAN?

SIMPLICITY ITSELF, CIMMERIAN...

BY *IMITATING* THE RIVER-DRAGONS, THE WATAMBIS HOPE TO BRING THEM HERE IN *SPIRIT.*

BY *NOW,* INFLUENCED BY THE *LIQUORS* THEY'VE DRUNK, THEY QUITE BELIEVE THEY *ARE* THE DRAGON-RIDERS!

YOU OLD *FAKIR*-- YOU'RE AS MUCH AT HOME IN THE INCENSE-BURNING TEMPLES OF *SHEM* AS IN ANY *JUNGLE.*

WHY DO THEY WANT THE RAIDERS TO *COME BACK*-- EVEN IN *SPIRIT*?

HOW ELSE TO *DEAL* WITH THEM, MY FRIEND?

WATCH *CLOSELY,* NOW--

--THE *GIRL* WHO NOW LEAPS UPON THE *STAGE* WHERE THE "DRAGON-RIDERS" MADLY DANCE!

SHE IS THE *CHIEF'S DAUGHTER*-- HER NAME, I BELIEVE, IS *NYAMI!*

MAWU!! KATONGI!!

SINCE THE CHIEF IS *OLD,* YET HAS *NO SONS*--

--SHE IS HIS *SUBSTITUTE* IN THIS RITUAL--

14

IF *SHE* DEFEATS THE *"DRAGON-RIDERS"*-- THEN SO WILL THE *TRIBE* DEFEAT THEM, WHEN NEXT THEY *CLASH.!*

DO YOU UNDERSTAND *NOW,* CIMMERIAN?

BUT, CONAN DOES NOT *ANSWER...*

...AS THE LOUDER, *EVER-LOUDER* POUNDING OF DRUMS AND CHANTING OF VOICES BEAT A RHYTHM THAT STIRS HIS VERY *BEING.*

TO THE *GIRL,* TOO, THIS RITUAL IS AS *REAL* AS ANY BATTLE.

CONAN CAN *SEE* THAT.

YET, OVERCOME WITH THE *WILD FRENZY* OF THEIR OWN WRITHING DANCE--

--THE FALSE DRAGON-RIDERS SEEM ABOUT TO *OVERWHELM* THEIR LITHESOME FOE--

--TILL THEY ARE *STARTLED* INTO SANITY BY A *CRY THAT ECHOES FROM HELL!*

HAII!!

THE GLAZE FADES FROM THE *GIRL'S* EYES, HOWEVER...

...ONLY WHEN THE NEWCOMER TEARS THE *SPEAR* FROM HER HAND...

...AND PUTS ITS *BLUNTER END* TO GOOD USE!

THAT MOON-MADDENED, DRUNKEN *FOOL!*

DOES HE WANT TO BRING THE *WHOLE TRIBE* DOWN UPON US HERE, IN THEIR OWN *VILLAGE*--

--AND *ALL* FOR DESIRE FOR THAT *VIXEN?*

STAY, BÊLIT! THE GIRL HAS LITTLE TO *DO* WITH IT...!

"IT IS THE *SPIRIT OF THE DANCE* THAT HAS MOVED THE SOUL OF YOUR *BARBARIAN LOVER.*

"IT IS THE *DANCE,* NOT LUST, THAT STIRS THEM THUS!

"SEE HOW THEY WRITHE WITH *WILD ABANDON* ABOUT THE FIRE?

AND THE WATAMBIS ARE HAPPY NOW, SENSING *VICTORY* IN THEIR NEXT BATTLE. THEY--

YET, EVEN A *MAN OF THE GODS* KNOWS WHEN HIS WORDS *FAIL* TO CONVINCE... SO HE LAPSES INTO *SILENCE.*

N'YAGA...

WHATEVER YOU *SAY,* MISTRESS.

...*MORE* OF THIS DEVIL'S BREW!

THE *CRUSHED POWDER* HE DROPS INTO BÊLIT'S BOWL, HOWEVER, IS N'YAGA'S *OWN* IDEA...

16

AND, IT SEEMS RATHER A **GOOD** ONE. FOR, SOON...

AHHH... YOU ARE **BACK**, MY LOVER...!

...THE "GODDESS" IS IN A FAR MORE **MELLOW** MOOD.

IT GROWS **LATE.**

AND **I** GROW... **SLEEPY.**

TOO SLEEPY... EVEN TO **WALK.**

THEN I'LL **CARRY** YOU.

CROM, BUT YOU'RE A -- **STRANGE** WOMAN-- READY TO **RAZE** A VILLAGE ONE MOMENT--

--OR LEAVE YOURSELF TO ITS **MERCIES** THE NEXT.

TO **YOUR** MERCY, CONAN-- ONLY **YOURS--!**

AS I SAID: A **STRANGE** WOMAN.

BUT THEN, THE KIND OF WOMAN EVEN A **SHOP-KEEPER** CAN PREDICT...

...WOULD PUT A **SATYR** TO SLEEP.

ERE LONG, THE **DRAGON-DANCE** NOW DONE, THE WATAMBIS STUMBLE OFF DROWZILY TO THEIR **HUTS**...

...SECURE IN THEIR BELIEF IN THE **MIGHTI-NESS** OF THEIR GREAT JUJU.

FOR, DOES NOT EVEN A **GODDESS**-- THE DAUGHTER OF DARK **DERKETA** HERSELF-- SLEEP AMONG THEM?

17

THE WATAMBIS' WINES ARE *POWERFUL* THINGS...

...YET, NOT POWER-FUL ENOUGH TO PREVENT *CONAN,* HOURS LATER, FROM FEELING THE *EARTH* TREMBLE EVER SO SLIGHTLY BENEATH HIS WEARY BODY...

...AS IF WITH THE LEADEN WEIGHT OF *GREAT TALONS.*

EVEN *BEFORE* HE CHARGES THRU THE DOOR OF THE DARKENED HUT, HE *KNOWS*--

--THAT THE *DRAGON-RIDERS* HAVE RETURNED!

AND *UNLUCKY* THE FIRST WATAMBI WHO HAS *ENCOUNTERED* THEM, WHILE STUMBLING TOWARD THE RIVER TO WASH HIS DIZZINESS AWAY!

AAIEEE!

AND, CHARGING INTO THEIR MIDST IN A *BLIND FURY*--

ARRRHH--!

--THE *SECOND* MAN TO SEE THEM IS SCARCELY MORE *FORTUNATE.*

GOOD THAT THE *FULL MOON* CASTS REPTILIAN SHADOWS UPON THE *DAZED* BARBARIAN...

...ELSE THE HUGE CROCODILE WOULD CHOMP DOWN ON MORE THAN A *SHRED OF LOINCLOTH* THIS NIGHT!

YET, *FEARFUL* THOUGH HE BE OF THINGS *SUPERNATURAL,* CONAN HAS BATTLED DRAGONS *LARGER* THAN THESE--

AND, AS HE TOLD *M'GORA*--

--IT'S ALL A MATTER OF *LEVERAGE!*

ON *LAND,* THE RIVER-DRAGONS ARE MORE USEFUL TO *FRIGHTEN* THAN TO *SLAY.*

STILL, THEY ARE FEARSOME *ENOUGH...*

AND, IT IS NOT TILL HE HEARS THAT GREAT NECK *SNAP*--

--NOT TILL HE FEELS THAT MASSIVE HEAD GROW SUDDENLY *LIMP* IN HIS STRAINING ARMS--

--THAT HE *RELAXES* HIS BONE-CRUSHING GRIP!

YET, BEFORE WEARY MUSCLES MAY RELAX, THEY *TENSE* AGAIN, AS CONAN WHIRLS--

--TO SEE N'YAGA, CORNERED BY ONE OF THE DREADED *DRAGON-RIDERS!*

STILL, TO *CORNER* THE TIGRESS' REVERED SHAMAN...

...IS NOT THE SAME AS *SLAYING* HIM.

AND, WHEN THE GLEAMING *POWDER* BURSTS INTO SHIMMERING *FLAME*...

GRUNK!

...IT IS THE *DRAGON-RIDER* WHO PAYS THE PRICE!

AAAA!

CHIEF OMBASSA AND HIS DAUGHTER, HOWEVER, HAVE *NO* MAGIC STUNTS TO PULL FROM THEIR GATHERED ROBES...

RUN, MY FATHER-- *RUN!*

WE *CANNOT!* WE CAN ONLY *STAND* --

--STAND AND *DIE* AS *WATAMBIS!*

20

YYY

WHITE-SKIN!

NO, OMBASSA! LIVE-- AND FIGHT!

THESE DEVILS ARE WELL-TRAINED -- AND I'VE DRIVEN HORSES A-PLENTY IN MY TIME.

CURSE ME FOR A HYPERBOREAN IF I DON'T THINK I CAN-- YES!

THE RIVER-DRAGONS HAVE BEEN TRAINED TO ATTACK-- TO KILL.

THEIR PREY IS ANYONE OR ANYTHING WHICH GETS IN THEIR PATH--

--EVEN EACH OTHER!

IN MOMENTS, IT IS A THREE-WAY, TWELVE-LIMBED BATTLE OF MONSTERS--

--AND CONAN TAKES HIS LEAVE, WITH A SINGLE PANTHERISH LEAP!

GRNGK!

DAGON'S MANHOOD! PERHAPS WE MAY PREVAIL, AFTER ALL!

WE WILL-- IF MY MEN KEEP THEIR WITS ABOUT THEM.

HO, YOU CORSAIRS-- YOU WOLVES OF THE SEA--

PROVE THAT YOU ARE WOLVES OF THE RIVER-BED AS WELL!

LOOSE YOUR ARROWS!

AND THE LONG DEADLY SHAFTS ARE LOOSED--

--IN A GREAT RAIN OF WOOD AND SHARP-CUT STONE!

A FEW MOMENTS' HESITATION...

...AND THE ATTACKERS FLEE, THE ELEMENT OF SURPRISE NO LONGER ON THEIR SIDE.

AI! IT IS JUJU!

THEY HAVE BEEN BEATEN OFF-- BY NOTHING MORE THAN SPEARS AND ARROWS?

THEY COUNTED FEAR THEIR GREATEST WEAPON, FOR THEY WERE FEW IN NUMBER.

FEAR FAILED THEM, SO-- WHAT'S THAT?

OHHHH--!

ONE OF THE DRAGON-RIDERS--

--WOUNDED, BUT STILL ALIVE!

NOT FOR LONG SHALL HE LIVE, WHITE-SKIN! STAND ASIDE, AND--

NO! DON'T YOU SEE?

WE CAN LEARN FROM THIS MAN--

--THOUGH ONLY IF WE HURRY!

HEAR ME! WHY DID YOU ATTACK THIS VILLAGE, WHEN YOU ALREADY LOOTED ITS IVORY?

TELL ME-- AND MY SHAMAN'S MEDICINE MAY HEAL YOUR WOUNDS.

HAD-- TO COME BACK--

GET SOMETHING-- ANYTHING--!

GET SLAVES! MAYBE THEY WOULD SATISFY-- THE ONE WE FEAR--

GET SLAVES-- FOR AMRA--!

AMRA!? WHO OR WHAT IN SEVEN HELLS IS THAT?

I NEVER HEARD THE WORD.

SPEAK UP, OR I'LL--

HE IS DEAD.

DO YOU KNOW ANYTHING OF THIS AMRA, WHOM EVEN THE DRAGON-RIDERS FEAR?

A LEGEND-- OF A WILD MAN WHO RUNS WITH THE GREAT CATS.

THE VERY NAME MEANS... LION!

WHITE-SKIN-- WE KNOW NOW WE CAN BEST OUR ENEMIES-- IF YOU WILL LEAD US--!

TONIGHT, YOU HAVE DRUNK OUR *WINE*-- DANCED OUR *JUJU!*

WILL YOU LEAD US AGAINST THE DRAGON- RIDERS?

NO, OMBASSA. IT IS *BÉLIT* WHO CHOOSES THE *BLACK CORSAIRS'* FOES-- AND SHE STICKS TO THE *SEA-PATHS.*

STILL, I *WONDER* WHY THE NOISE OF THE *ATTACK* DID NOT--

THEN, STEPPING *INSIDE* THE NIGHT-DARK HUT, CONAN WONDERS *NO LONGER...*

FOR, THERE IS *NOTHING THERE...*

...BUT A TORN *NECKLACE...*

...FASHIONED OF THE *TEETH OF CROCODILES!*

WHITE-SKIN... *WHAT*--?

NOW, OMBASSA. *NOW* I WILL LEAD THE WATAMBIS AGAINST THE *DRAGON- RIDERS!*

AND THERE'LL BE *NO REST* FOR ME, IN *HEAVEN* OR ON *EARTH*--

--TILL *EVERY ONE* OF THEM WRITHES BLEEDING IN THE LOATHSOME *PITS OF HELL!!*

TO BE CONTINUED...

23

"Know, O prince, that between the years when the oceans drank Atlantis and the gleaming cities, and the rise of the sons of Aryas, there was an Age undreamed of, when shining kingdoms lay spread across the world like blue mantles beneath the stars.
"Hither came Conan, the Cimmerian, black-haired, sullen-eyed, sword in hand, a thief, a reaver, a slayer, with gigantic melancholies and gigantic mirth, to tread the jeweled thrones of the Earth under his sandaled feet."

—*The Nemedian Chronicles.*

EARLIER, OMBASSA, I SPOKE AS A FOOL!

I THOUGHT YOUR QUARREL WAS NOT OURS-- BECAUSE YOU DWELL ON LAND, WHILE WE PLY THE WESTERN SEA!

YET, EVEN AS WE FOUGHT OFF YOUR ENEMIES' RAID, THEY STOLE THE WOMAN I LOVE--

AND, BY CROM, I'LL HAVE HER BACK--

--AYE, AND MAKE THE DRAGON-RIDERS PAY FOR THEIR DEVILTRY, AS WELL!

THERE ARE FEW NOBLER ACTS THAN TO DO BATTLE FOR ONE'S HEARTH OR ONE'S MATE...

--THE MORE SO WHEN SHE IS A GODDESS AS WELL, AS BELIT IS!

BUT, IN THE NAME OF DAGON--DO NOT GO ALONE INTO THE BUSH!

YOU COME FROM A FAR-OFF LAND, AND DO NOT KNOW THE JUNGLE WAYS!

MY DAUGHTER SPEAKS WISELY, WHITE-SKIN!

YOU MUST TAKE SOME MEN OF THE WATAM-BIS WITH YOU!

FOR, WE ALSO HAVE OUR PRIDE--AND THE DEFEAT OF THE DRAGON-RIDERS MUST BE OUR VICTORY, TOO!

DONE! I'LL TAKE A HANDFUL OF YOUR TRIBES-MEN, IF ONLY TO GUIDE ME.

MY CORSAIRS WILL WAIT ON BOARD OUR SHIP, UNTIL--

NO!

WHAT DID YOU SAY, KAWAKU?

I SAY--LET US SAIL, AND LEAVE OUR CAPTAIN TO HER FATE!

IF SHE IS TRULY THE DAUGHTER OF THE DEATH-GODDESS DERKETA, AS SHE CLAIMS, SHE IS IN NO DANGER--

--AND IF SHE IS NOT, THEN WHAT NEED HAVE WE OF A WOMAN CAPTAIN?

BY THE GODS! THAT TREACHER-OUS--

KAWAKU WAS EVER ENVIOUS OF BELIT--NO DOUBT BECAUSE HE ONCE SAT HIGH IN THE COUNCILS OF UZUMI, WHOM SHE OVERTHREW! I'LL--

STAY, M'GORA!

BEST THAT HE WHO IS OUR CAPTAIN'S LOVER HANDLE THIS!

AND, BY DAGON, I THINK HE **WILL!**

KEEP BACK, WHITE MAN!

KAWAKU DOES NOT FEAR YOU, LIKE THESE **OTHER** CRINGING DOGS!

I GAVE YOU AN **ORDER**, KAWAKU.

OBEY IT, OR I'LL STRIKE YOU DOWN LIKE THE **JACKAL** YOU ARE!

YOU **DARE** TO SPEAK THUS TO ME--

--WHILE MY **SPEAR** BRINGS FORTH A **TRICKLE OF BLOOD** --AND IS POISED TO PIERCE YOUR VERY **HEART?**

CONAN SAYS NO MORE...

...EXCEPT WITH STEEL-BLUE, ICE-COLD **EYES**...

...EYES WHICH SEEM TO **FREEZE** THE SPEAR-HAND OF HIS ANTAGONIST, JUST FOR A **MOMENT.**

YET, THAT MOMENT MIGHT AS WELL BE--

--**FOREVER.**

NOW, KAWAKU-- I SHOULD **RUN YOU THRU**--

BUT, IF I **REPEAT** MY COMMAND--

--WILL YOU **OBEY** IT THIS TIME?

I-- I **WILL!**

GOOD! THEN GET YOU BACK TO THE **TIGRESS**, WHERE SHE LIES AT **ANCHOR**--

--AND GIVE THANKS TO ALL YOUR **SOUTHERN GODS** --

--THAT OUR CREW IS SHORT ON **SPEARMEN!**

27

...WELL, N'YAGA? DO YOU THINK YOU AND M'GORA CAN HOLD THEM IN LINE TILL I *RETURN*?

YOU KNOW FULL WELL THEY ALL BUT *WORSHIP* BÊLIT, CONAN--AND WHY *NOT*?

FOR, DID I NOT *ARRANGE* THINGS SO THAT SHE EVER SEEMED A *GODDESS* TO THEM?

I'VE ALWAYS *WONDERED* ABOUT THAT.

WHY DID YOU DO THAT, WHEN YOU COULD HAVE USED YOUR *TRICKS* TO MAKE *YOURSELF* RULER OF THE SOUTHERN ISLES, *INSTEAD*?

WHO IN HIS RIGHT MIND WANTS TO BE A *KING*, WHEN HE CAN BE THE POWER *BEHIND* THE THRONE?

HERE-- DRINK THIS *BREW*.

FOUL-SMELLING STUFF! *WHAT--*

YOU ARE *STRONG*, CONAN--BUT THE *JUNGLE* HAS ILLNESSES TO LAY YOU LOW AS ANY *SICKLY GIRL* WITHOUT IT!

DRINK IT--AS I MADE *BÊLIT* DO, WHEN SHE WAS KNEE-HIGH TO A *CRICKET*.

AND NOW, THE *WATAMBIS* AWAIT....!

THE BLESSINGS OF OUR *GODS* FALL UPON YOUR SHOULDERS, WHITE-SKIN!

THE TRIBESMEN WHO GO *WITH* YOU WILL NOT *DESERT* YOU--NO, NOT IF THEY FACE *DEATH* ITSELF AT YOUR SIDE!

I'VE SPENT *LITTLE* TIME YET IN THE JUNGLE...

THAT'S GOOD-- BECAUSE THEY DOUBTLESS *WILL*!

...BUT ALREADY, IT SEEMS TO ME THAT EVERYTHING HERE *LIVES* SOLELY BY PREYING UPON *SOMETHING ELSE*...

...ONLY TO *DIE*, IN ITS *TURN*.

THE DAYS THAT FOLLOW ARE *LONG*, AND *HARD* AND STEAMING *HOT*.

THEY ARE FILLED WITH *RIDERLESS* CROCODILES-- AND WITH GREAT GROTESQUE BEASTS THE WATAMBIS CALL *RIVER-CATTLE*.

THEY ARE FILLED, ALSO, WITH PRECARIOUSLY-SWAYING *BRIDGES*, WHICH CROSS AND RE-CROSS THE GENTLY FLOWING *RIVER*...

...WITH DENSE, CLOYING *VEGETATION* WHICH CLINGS ALMOST LIKE A *THING ALIVE*...

...AND WITH EVEN *DENSER* CLOUDS OF STINGING *INSECTS*, WHICH AT TIMES FORCE THE PARTY INTO REPTILE-LADEN *WATERS* TO ESCAPE.

AT SUCH MOMENTS, CONAN RECALLS THE *BITTER BREW* WHICH N'YAGA FORCED UPON HIM ERE HE'D LEFT THE *VILLAGE*...

AND, IN HIS MEMORY, ALREADY IT TASTES FAR *SWEETER* THAN IT DID BEFORE.

THERE ARE STEEP *CLIFFS*, TOO, WHICH CONAN SCALES MORE *EASILY* THAN HIS COMPANIONS...

...GIVING HIM TIME TO *THINK* AND *REFLECT*.

AND, AS THEY *TREK ON*, DAY AND NIGHT...

...HIS THOUGHTS GO BACK AGAIN AND AGAIN TO THE *OBJECT* OF HIS VENGEFUL QUEST:

BÊLIT, QUEEN OF THE BLACK COAST!

WHY, HE WONDERS, DOES *THIS* GIRL MEAN MORE TO HIM THAN *OTHERS* WHO HAVE CROSSED HIS WANDERING PATH?

IN SUCH MOMENTS, HE *THINKS* OF THE WOMEN HE HAS MET AMONG THE *CIVILIZED PEOPLES*, SINCE LEAVING HIS NATIVE *CIMMERIA*:

OF *RED SONJA*, HYRKANIAN-BORN SHE-DEVIL WHO COULD OUTDRINK A NEMEDIAN, OUTSWEAR A ZINGARAN, AND OUT-DUEL A POITANIAN KNIGHT -- YET WHOSE *HEART* WAS AS COLD TOWARD MEN AS THE *NORTHERN SNOWS*;

OF *JENNA*, WHO TAUGHT HIM THAT A WOMAN MAY SMILE WITH HER EYES, WHILE SHE LIES WITH HER LIPS -- OR *VICE VERSA*;

OF *AMYTIS*, WHOSE ACCO[L] HE FLED *TURAN*, WITH BOTH MEN AN[D] WERE-DEMON[S] AT HIS HEELS.

...OF MELISSANDRA, QUEEN OF NOW-FALLEN MAKKALET, WHO MIGHT HAVE RIDDEN AT HIS SIDE--IF SHE'D NOT HAD DUTIES TO HER UNBORN HEIR;

...OF A FAR LESS ADMIRABLE QUEEN, ONE FATIMA OF ZAHMANN, WHO TRIED TO TURN HIM INTO A HOUSEHOLD CUR-- ONLY TO LEARN SHE'D TAKEN A WOLF INTO HER BOUDOIR INSTEAD;

YES, MANY HAVE BEEN THE WOMEN IN HIS NIGH-TWO-SCORE YEARS.

AYE, AND OF STRANGER, NIGH-UNHUMAN WOMEN, WHO YET HAUNT HIS LESS-GUARDED NIGHTS:

WOMEN WITH NAMES LIKE UATHACHT--AND ZEPHRA--AND ATALI, DAUGHTER OF THE FROST-GIANT YMIR-- AND ZHADORR, WHO CAME SPORE-LIKE FROM THE HEAVENS--AYE, AND EVEN A NAMELESS SHADOW-WOMAN WHO EXISTED ONLY IN A STRANGE, HIGH, MIST-SHROUDED TOWER 'TWIXT OPHIR AND MESSANTIA.

YET, NONE HAS TOUCHED HIS VERY BEING, OR SEEMED MORE THE MATE OF HIS SOUL, THAN THIS BELIT--

--SHE WHOSE VERY NAME MEANS GODDESS!

31

AND, EVEN AS HER *FACE* ABRUPTLY FLOATS BEFORE HIM, BLOTTING OUT, *ENGULFING* ALL THE OTHERS LIKE A GREAT DARK *FLAME*--HE MUSES:

HE'S SAID HE *LOVES* THIS GIRL. HE'S MADE A WOMAN.

COULD IT JUST POSSIBLY BE THAT HE *MEANT* WHAT HE SAID?

AND MEANWHILE, SOME LEAGUES UP-RIVER, HER THOUGHTS ARE LIKE-WISE OF *HIM*...

...TILL A *HATED VOICE* ALREADY GROWN FAMILIAR BRINGS HER BACK TO A HARSH, UNYIELDING *REALITY*:

MAY DAGON *DAMN* THESE WRETCHED BEASTS FOR THE *SLUGS* THEY TRULY ARE!

PROD YOUR MOUNTS *ONWARD*, DEVIL-BROTHERS--

FOR, EACH MOMENT WE *DELAY*, WE RISK THE FURTHER WRATH OF *AMRA!*

WHO *IS* THIS "*AMRA*" I'VE HEARD YOU MENTION?

YOUR VOICE *TREMBLES* WHEN YOU SPEAK OF HIM, AS IF HE WERE A VERY *DEMON!*

BUT THEN, I SUSPECT YOU FEAR *MANY* THINGS! WHY ELSE DID YOU GO *SKULKING ABOUT* TO CAPTURE ME IN MY *SLEEP*, WHILE YOUR LACKEYS CARRIED THE BRUNT OF *BATTLE*?

GIVE ME A *SPEAR*, AND PERHAPS I CAN *PROTECT* YOU FROM-- *UNNNH!*

SHUT YOUR MOUTH, WOMAN!!

YOU ARE *BRAVE*, FELLOW-- WHEN DEALING WITH SOMEONE *TIGHTLY BOUND* WITH THONGS!

I WANT TO BE AROUND WHEN YOU STAND TREMBLING BEFORE THIS *AMRA* YOU FEAR!

WE ARE *THEY WHO RIDE THE RIVER-DRAGONS* ...AND WE FEAR *NO ONE!*

OH--?

THEN, TELL ME WHY YOUR SO-CALLED "*WARRIORS*" GROW WIDE-EYED AND *SHAKING* AT THE MERE MENTION OF THE NAME *AMRA!*

AMRA, I SAY-- AND *AGAIN-- AMRA!*

QUIET, WOMAN-- OR I SHALL *FORGET* THAT YOU ARE MARKED TO BE THE *BRIDE OF AMRA*--

--AND WE SHALL HAVE A BIT LESS *FOOD* TO GATHER TO FEED OUR *MOUNTS!*

YOU *PRATTLE* FOOLISHLY, WOMAN-LIKE, OF THINGS YOU *DO NOT KNOW!*

YOU HAVE NEVER HEARD THE *ROAR OF AMRA* SPLITTING THE JUNGLE NIGHT MORE *FEARSOME* EVEN THAN THAT OF THE *GREAT CATS* WHICH RUN WITH HIM!

"NOR HAVE YOU HAD MEN *SLAIN IN AMBUSH* BY A PRIDE OF CLAWING *LIONS*, LED BY THAT *GREAT BLACK BEAST* WHICH MANY SAY IS *AMRA HIMSELF*, IN FOUR-LEGGED, MANY-TALONED FORM!"

"WHEN THEY *ATTACK* THUS, THEY OVERCOME THEIR FEAR OF *MEN*--OF *SPEARS*--AYE, EVEN OF *FIRE!*"

"AGAINST SUCH *DEVIL-CREATURES*, WHO CAN *STAND?*"

"CERTAINLY NOT OUR HAPLESS SENTRIES, WHO WERE OFTEN PICKED OFF AT NIGHT, AS EASILY AS IF THEY HAD BEEN OLD, DEAF WOMEN.

"SOMETIMES WE FOUND THEM WITH THE MARK OF A MAN'S HANDS ON THEIR THROATS, OR KNIFE-HOLES IN THEIR GULLETS...

"...JUST AS OFTEN, THEIR BODIES SHREDDED BY THE CLAWS OF LIONS THAT NEVER ROARED."

A PRETTY TALE-- AND ONE THAT GLADDENS MY HEART TO HEAR!

TELL ME-- HAVE YOU EVER SEEN THIS AMRA?

ONLY FROM AFAR!

ONLY WELL ENOUGH TO KNOW THAT HE HAS PALE SKIN--

-- SO THAT YOU WILL BE, WE HOPE, A WELCOME PRIZE FOR HIM, AND HE WILL LEAVE US ALONE FOR A TIME!

PERHAPS I SHOULD THANK YOU FOR THE COMPLIMENT, DOG--

--BUT I PREFER TO SAY GOOD-BYE!

I'LL SEE YOU IN HELL!

DAGON'S MANHOOD! THE WITCH IS FREE!

STOP HER! STOP HER!

AYE, O CHIEFTAIN-- BUT, SHE SWIMS LIKE NO MAN OR WOMAN EVER SEEN!

LOOK! ALREADY SHE GAINS THE SHORE!

THEN CHASE HER ON THE SHORE, FOOLS!

WE WILL ALL SUFFER, AT THE HANDS OF AN ANGRY AMRA--

--IF WE BRING HIM NEITHER IVORY, NOR SLAVES, NOR BRIDE!

AFTER HER, I SAY!

BUT, *BÊLIT* HAS BEEN *RAISED* IN JUNGLES SUCH AS THIS, ON THE FAR-OFF *SOUTHERN ISLES*...

AND, *UNFAMILIAR* THOUGH THIS COUNTRY BE TO HER, SHE SOON *FADES* INTO IT LIKE A PHANTOM *MIST*...

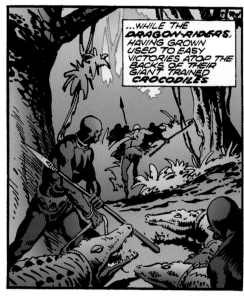

...WHILE THE *DRAGON-RIDERS*, HAVING GROWN USED TO EASY VICTORIES ATOP THE BACKS OF THEIR GIANT TRAINED *CROCODILES*

...HAVE BEEN ABLE TO SPARE *LITTLE* TIME FOR HONING THEIR SKILLS UPON THE VINE-ENTANGLED LAND...

...SO THAT THOSE WHO *SCOUR* THE JUNGLE MUST SOON RETURN *EMPTY-HANDED*...

...TO A *CHIEFTAIN* WILLING TO BLAME ANY SAVE *HIMSELF* FOR THE DAY'S BRIGHT FOLLY.

AND SOON, AS A GREAT *FIRE* ROARS A SAFE DISTANCE FROM THE TETHERED REPTILES, THEY HAVE ALREADY *FORGOTTEN* THE WOMAN, AND LAY PLANS INSTEAD TO TRY AGAIN TO *TRAP* THE MAN-DEVIL CALLED *AMRA.*

WITH SUCH *LIES* AND *FALSE HOPES* THEY PASS THE FULL-MOONED NIGHT...

...WHILE THEIR **ONCE-PREY**, ALREADY ASSIGNED TO OBLIVION, CONTINUES TO **FLEE**, CASTING GRIM GLANCES OVER SUPPLE SHOULDERS.

BY THE TIME SHE IS CERTAIN SHE IS NO LONGER **FOLLOWED**, SHE IS ALREADY **FAR** FROM THE ON-FLOWING RIVER.

INSTINCTIVELY, SHE HEADS FOR THE **HIGHEST PINNACLE** SHE CAN REACH IN THE DARK--A PLACE WHERE SHE CAN FEEL **SAFE**--

--ALTHOUGH SHE KNOWS ENOUGH OF JUNGLES TO REALIZE ONE CAN **NEVER** FEEL SAFE THERE, NOT EVEN **FULLY ARMED**.

AND SHE IS **WEAPONLESS**.

BUT, ERE LONG, EVEN **WARY EYES** CANNOT ESCAPE THE SPELL OF **MORFI**, KUSHITE GOD OF SLEEP...

...OR OF HIS **MATE KMRA**, WHO SPRINKLES BOTH GENTLE DREAMS AND NIGHTMARES FROM THE POUCH UPON HER SIDE.

MEANWHILE, THE **DRAGON-RIDERS** ARE ABOUT TO LEARN THAT IT IS NEITHER BÊLIT **NOR** AMRA THAT SHOULD HAVE CONCERNED THEM

CROM'S DEVILS! THE DOGS FEEL **SAFE**, DOUBTING ANY WOULD BE BRAVE ENOUGH TO **PURSUE** THEM!

THAT WILL MAKE IT ALL THE EASIER FOR ME TO GET **NEAR** THEM ALONE...

...THOUGH, IN TRUTH, I'D SOONER THEY'D LEFT A **SENTRY** WITH A **THROAT** RIPE FOR SLITTING!

HE IS *NEW* TO THE JUNGLE--YET HE MOVES AS QUIETLY AS ANY CIMMERIAN *HILL-PANTHER*, THANKING THE UNCARING GODS THERE IS NO *WIND* TO CARRY HIS SCENT TO THE *DRAGONS*.

CIRCLING THE CAMP, HE LIVES A THIN TRAIL OF *POWDER* BEHIND HIM, FROM THE VIAL GIVEN HIM BY *N'YAGA*...

...EVEN MANAGING TO CUT OFF THE *SLUMBERING* CROCODILES FROM THEIR BELOVED *RIVER*.

T*HE REMAINDER* OF HIS ABLUTIONS TAKE ONLY A FEW SHORT *MOMENTS*...

A*ND* SUDDENLY, THE NIGHT BURSTS INTO *LIVID BRIGHTNESS* WHICH ALL BUT DROWNS THE VERY *MOON!*

AIEEEE! DAGON HELP US!

FIRE! FIRE ALL AROUND US--!

T*HEN,* AS THE FRIGHTEN-ED RAIDERS MILL *ABOUT* IN STARK FEAR--

--THE *REPTILES*, EVEN MORE TERRIFIED OF THE FIRE, TRAMPLE THEM AND EACH OTHER IN THEIR MAD DASH TO REACH THE SAFETY OF TEPID *WATERS!*

NOT NEARLY ALL OF THEM MAKE IT--

AND, CONAN AND HIS WATAMBIS SEE NO MEN AT ALL LEAVE THAT RING OF WITHERING FIRE.

YET, ALL THE WHILE, THE TRIBESMEN RAIN ARROW AFTER ARROW UPON THE SCENE...

AT LAST, THE FIRES DIE-- AND A FEW HARD-HIDED, BADLY-SCORCHED DRAGONS CRAWL DAZEDLY INTO THE WAITING RIVER--

--LEAVING BEHIND THEM THOSE WHO WERE ONCE THEIR MASTERS, AND WHO WITH THE DAWN MAY BE THEIR MEALS.

QUICKLY, BROTHERS!

YOU KNOW WHAT TO DO!

HERE, WHITE-SKIN! HERE IS ONE WHO IS ALIVE!

MITRA! I RECOGNIZE HIM! HE WAS THEIR LEADER IN THE RAID ON YOUR VILLAGE!

HE SEEMS OVERCOME BY THE SMOKE AND HEAT-- BUT THERE ARE FEW MARKS OF THE FIRE UPON HIM!

YOU HAVE DONE WELL, ANAKI!

SPEAK, DOG! WHERE IS THE WOMAN YOU STOLE FROM THE HUT OF THE WATAMBIS?

I-I SWEAR-- I DO NOT KNOW!

SHE ESCAPED--FLED INTO THE JUNGLE, LONG BEFORE THE FALL OF NIGHT--!

THEN YOU WILL HELP US FIND HER--

--WHILE PRAYING TO YOUR GODS THAT WE FIND HER ALIVE!

MEANWHILE, SOME FEW LEAGUES DISTANT, A *VAST DARK SHAPE* FLITS BETWEEN EARTH AND THE MOON'S WIDE-STARING EYE...

...TOWARD A *STILL, WHITE FORM* WHICH SPRAWLS IN VIVID *CONTRAST* TO THE BLACKNESS ALL ABOUT HER.

MAMMOTH WINGS BEAT CALMLY, SILENTLY, SENDING A SOOTHING BREEZE ACROSS THE SLEEPER'S FACE...

...TILL SHE *WAKES* ABRUPTLY, TO FEEL THE GRASPING OF *COLD, HARD TALONS,* AND TO SEE--

BY ISHTAR!

SHE WASTES NO MORE BREATH NOW ON WORDS--

--BUT *HOLDS* FOR DEAR LIFE TO THE RUGGED *ROOT* BENEATH HER--

UNNNHH...!

--AS THE MONSTROUS *MOTH-DEMON* ALL BUT PULLS HER ARM FROM ITS SOCKET TRYING TO RISE *SKYWARD.*

THEN, IT TURNS--AND FROM HIS GAPING MAW A WARMISH, STICKY *LIQUID* IS HURLED--

--*ENWRAPPING* HER, AS IT MUST HAVE DONE TO MANY AN *ANTELOPE* OR *FAWN*--!

BUT, THIS IS *NO SMALL* FRIGHTENED *ANIMAL* IT HAS CHOSEN FOR ITS QUARRY.

THIS IS BÊLIT--AND SHE IS SOMETHING QUITE *DIFFERENT!*

THE **FORCE** OF THE BLOW, COMBINED WITH THE GIRL'S WEIGHT, BRINGS THE GREAT INSECT HURTLING TO **EARTH**--

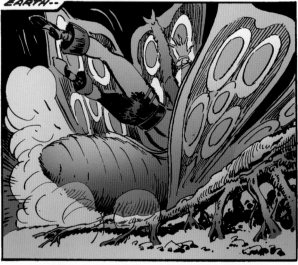

--WHERE AN **EERIE TABLEAU** IS ENACTED, AND THE ILL-MATCHED BATTLE **RAGES ON!**

YET, THE **OUTCOME** IS NEVER REALLY IN **DOUBT**...

SLOWLY, INEXORABLY, BÊLIT IS DRAWN **NEARER** AND **NEARER** THOSE CLICKING, SLAVERING JAWS--

--UNTIL, **SUDDENLY**--WITHOUT A SOUND OF **WARNING**--

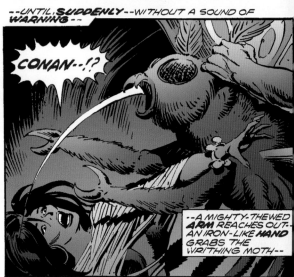

CONAN--!?

--A MIGHTY-THEWED **ARM** REACHES OUT-- AN IRON-LIKE **HAND** GRABS THE WRITHING MOTH--

--AND, WITH A SINGLE, SWIFT MOTION, **ANOTHER** POWERFUL ARM DRIVES A **SHARP, GLEAMING BLADE** THRU THE CREATURE'S MOST VULNERABLE PART, **SEVERING** IT.

ITS **WINGS** CONTINUE TO FLUTTER, OF COURSE--AS IF TO SPEED **DEPARTING LIFE** ON ITS WAY.

THEN, WHEN THE MOTH'S **SHADOW** NO LONGER HIDES THE **RESCUER** BEYOND--

ISHTAR TAKE ME!

YOU'RE-- **NOT** CONAN! THEN **WHO**--??

"Know, O prince, that between the years when the oceans drank Atlantis and the gleaming cities, and the rise of the sons of Aryas, there was an Age undreamed of, when shining kingdoms lay spread across the world like blue mantles beneath the stars.
"Hither came Conan, the Cimmerian, black-haired, sullen-eyed, sword in hand, a thief, a reaver, a slayer, with gigantic melancholies and gigantic mirth, to tread the jeweled thrones of the Earth under his sandaled feet."
—The Nemedian Chronicles.

STAN LEE PRESENTS: CONAN THE BARBARIAN™

LORD OF THE LIONS!

"WART HOG!"

IN THE MODERN WORLD, OR IN THE DANGER-LADEN HYBORIAN AGE: A CRY TO CHILL THE VERY SOUL-- AND FREEZE MEN'S BLOOD IN THROBBING VEINS--

CROM'S DEVILS!

AIEEEE

GRONK

ANOTHER EXCURSION INTO STRANGE WORLDS OF SWORDS AND SORCERY BY:
ROY THOMAS & JOHN BUSCEMA
AUTHOR & EDITOR   ARTIST
STEVE GAN EMBELLISHER
CONDOY LETTERER

FEATURING THE CREATIONS OF ROBERT E. HOWARD

CONAN IS FROM A COLDER, *NORTHERN* CLIMATE, WHERE THE GREATEST LIVING MENACE IS FROM LONG-CLAWED *BEARS* AND FUR-COVERED *HILL-PANTHERS*...

YET, EVEN *HE*, FULLY AS WELL AS THE JUNGLE-BORN *WATAMBI WARRIORS* WITH HIM, HAS HEARD TALES OF *THIS* MADDENED MASS OF TUSK AND FURY...

CLIMB, WATAMBIS! *CLIMB!*

...AND HE'S *NOT* ONE UNDULY EAGER TO FACE A FOE THERE'S NO *PROFIT* IN FIGHTING!

STAY THERE AND ROOT AMONG THE *TREE-TRUNKS*, YOU HAIRY DEVIL!

SNORT SNORT

YOU'LL SOON *TIRE* OF THE SPORT, AND GO YOUR *WAY!*

W-WHY DON'T YOU HURL YOUR *SWORD* AT HIM, WHITE-SKIN?

BE GLAD I DON'T FEED *YOU* TO HIM, DOG! AND I *WOULD*, TO PAY YOU BACK FOR LEADING YOUR *DRAGON-RIDERS* AGAINST US--

--AND CARRYING OFF *BÊLIT--*

--EXCEPT THAT I *NEED* YOU TO HELP US *FIND* HER AGAIN!

HAH! ALREADY, THE HOG SNIFFS *ANOTHER* TREE!

SOON, HE'LL GROW *BORED*, SINCE HE'S NO *MEAT-EATER*...

THEN, YOU CAN TAKE US TO THE SPOT WHERE THE *SHE-PIRATE* ESCAPED YOU, SO WE CAN--

I'LL TAKE YOU *NOWHERE*, WHITE-HUED JACKAL--

-- SINCE YOU WILL DIE *HERE--*

--UNNNNH--

43

--WHILE *I* MAKE MY *ESCAPE!*

BUT, EVEN AS HIS CAPTIVE LEAPS TO THE GROUND, CONAN CATCHES HIMSELF ON A STURDY VINE...

...SO THAT, NEXT INSTANT, THE SHARP-SCENTED WART HOG HAS BUT ONE POSSIBLE TARGE FOR HIS RAMPAGING WRATH

--*TINDAGA, ONCE CHIEFTAIN OF THE MUCH-FEARED RIDERS OF THE RIVER-DRAGONS*

GRONK

NO! IN THE NAME OF ALL THE *GODS*--

NNOOOOO!

WHITE-SKIN! SHALL I PUT THE FOOL OUT OF HIS *MISERY?*

NO, ANAKI--

THROW ME YOUR KNIFE! *HURRY!*

THAT SCHEMING DOG IS WORTH *TIME* TO ME IN FINDING MY *WOMAN*--

--OR ELSE I'D TAKE *PLEASURE* IN WATCHING HIS *DEATH-THROES!*

IN THE NAME OF *DAGON*-- *HELP ME!*

IMPACT:

THE SHARP METAL BLADE DIGS DEEP INTO THE BOAR'S BROAD NECK, BARELY MISSING THE SPINAL CORD...

AGAIN--

--*AND YET AGAIN*--

--*THE SNARLING CIMMERIAN STABS AT THE BLOOD-MAD BRUTE*--

44

YET, NO SHARP THRUST SEEMS TO STRIKE A *VITAL ORGAN* BENEATH THE WART HOG'S LEATHERY HIDE--

--AS IT *DRAGS* THE STRUGGLING BARBARIAN ALONG THE JUNGLE FLOOR--

THEN, NEXT MOMENT, A RAGGEDLY PROJECTING *TREE BOLE* SENDS THE *STARS* SPINNING 'ROUND IN CONAN'S HEAD

ARRRR

--AND, WORSE LUCK YET-- THE *KNIFE* FLYING FROM HIS HAND!

AMAZING THAT A BEAST WEIGHING NIGH *HALF A TON* CAN STOP SO *SHORT*--TURN SO *QUICKLY!*

BUT, CONAN HAS LITTLE TIME TO *MARVEL* AT NATURE'S WONDERS-

--AS HE SPIES HIS *FALLEN SWORD* LYING JUST OUT OF REACH!

THANKS BE TO CROM!

HE SCARCELY *HEARS* HIS OWN CRY, HOWEVER--OR HIS *GRUNT OF PAIN*--OVER THE THUNDERING ROAR OF *CLOVEN HOOVES*--

--AS HE *LEAPS* FOR THE GLEAMING BLADE--

--GRASPS ITS HARD, HEAVEN-SENT *HANDLE*--

--AND *RISES*, TO FACE THE HEAD-LONG CHARGE OF A CREATURE SPAWNED IN *HELL*--

--AND *MIDWIVED* IN THE STEAMING, DEADLY JUNGLES *SOUTH OF KUSH!*

COME *AHEAD* NOW, YOU LONG-TOOTHED *PIG*--!

COME ON AND GET--

--YOUR--

--SUPPER!

WHITE-SKIN-- YOU HAVE *SLAIN* THE *TUSK-HOG!*

TRULY, YOU ARE A *MIGHTY WARRIOR*--A FIT MATE FOR THE *STOLEN GODDESS* YOU SEEK!

WHY THEN DID NEITHER YOU NOR SHE TELL US YOUR *NAME?*

I AM OF A *FAR-OFF LAND,* MEN OF THE *WATAMBIS!*

MY NAME WOULD MEAN *NOTHING* TO YOU...

...NOR HAVE I THE *RIGHT* TO ANY NAME, TILL I'VE RECOVERED MY *WOMAN!*

BUT, WHITE-SKIN... THE DRAGON-RIDERS WERE TAKING HER TO BE THE *BRIDE* OF *AMRA*--HE WHOM THEY CALL *LORD OF THE LIONS!*

WHAT IF THE WILD *JUNGLE* BETWEEN HIS LAND AND OURS-- HAS ALREADY *CLAIMED* HER?

THEN I'LL BEAR *NO* NAME, ANAKI...TILL THE *END OF MY DAYS!*

SOON, SEVERAL MEN CARRY THEIR *SLAIN COMRADE* BACK TOWARD THEIR SEA-COAST *VILLAGE...*

...WHILE, *TINDAGA* AGAIN FIRMLY IN TOW, CONAN AND THE OTHERS CONTINUE THEIR SEARCH FOR *BÊLIT.*

BÊLIT: SHEMITISH SHE-PIRATE WHO, TAKEN FROM A WATAMBI HUT BY NIGHT, *ESCAPED* THE DRAGON-RIDERS' CLUTCHES--

46

AMRA!

I AM -- AMRA!

EYES OF *ISHTAR*! THEN-- THE HAND THAT SLEW THE *GIANT MOTH* WHICH ATTACKED ME--

--WAS THAT OF THE *VERY MAN-DEMON* TO WHOM THE RAIDERS WERE *TAKING* ME!

BUT-- THAT GREAT *BLACK LION* AT YOUR SIDE--

YES! THE *CHIEF* OF THE *DRAGON-RIDERS* SWORE YOU *TURNED INTO* SUCH A BEAST--!

THE DRAGON-RIDERS ARE *SPINELESS HYENAS*

I LET THEM *THINK* THEY RULE THE RIVER-BEDS, BECAUSE THEY BRING ME-- *THINGS I WANT!*

THIS NIGHT, THEY HAVE BROUGHT ME ... *YOU!*

HOW COULD YOU *KNOW* THAT, UNLESS-- BY *ASHTORETH!*

YOU WERE *TRAILING* US, ALL *ALONG!*

WHY HAVE YOU--?

BUT-- WHO *ARE* YOU?

THERE IS *NO TIME* FOR TALK NOW!

COME! WE GO TO THE *LAIR OF LIONS!*

THERE, YOU WILL BECOME *AMRA'S MATE* ... AND *RULE THE JUNGLE* AT MY SIDE!

THE DEVIL, I WILL!

JUST POINT ME THE WAY BACK TOWARD THE WATAMBI VILLAGE, AND I'LL--

BÉLIT IS NO SQUEAMISH, CITY-BRED COURTESAN, TO CRY OUT IN FEAR EVEN AT THE SIGHT OF AN ATTACKING LION--

SHULO! NO!!

YET, SHE IS STARTLED TO SEE THE MAN CALLED AMRA THRUST HIS VERY HANDS INTO THE BEAST'S MANE--

--AND MORE STARTLED STILL TO HEAR HIM ANSWER THE LION'S SNARLS--WITH HIS OWN--

--SNARLS NO MORE HUMAN THAN THE LION'S!

AFTER AN INSTANT, IT IS THE GREAT CAT WHICH TURNS AWAY--BEFORE ITS MASTER.

GO, SHULO!

GO! AMRA COMMANDS!

I AM SORRY! HE THOUGHT YOU MEANT TO STRIKE ME!

HE MAY YET BE PROVEN RIGHT! NOW, WHICH WAY IS IT TO--?

I HAVE SAID--WE HAVE NO TIME FOR FOOLISH TALK!

WE MUST REACH THE LAIR OF LIONS BEFORE THE DAY BREAKS!

AND I HAVE SAID-- GO TO SOME JUNGLE HELL, INSTEAD! I--

OHHHH--!

AMRA'S GRIP IS STRONG...

...AS STRONG PERHAPS AS CONAN'S, SHE CANNOT HELP THINKING--EVEN AS THE MAN-LION PULLS HER TO HIM--

--AND COVERS HER FULL RED LIPS WITH *KISSES!*

FOR A *FLEETING* MOMENT, IT IS AS IF SHE IS *BACK* ON BOARD THE *TIGRESS*-- IN *CONAN'S* ARMS--

AND THEN--SHE *REMEMBERS!*

YOU FILTHY *DUNG-DOG!*

LET-- ME-- GO!!

;ARRRN--!; YOU-- *STRUCK* AMRA!?

NO ONE STRIKES *AMRA!*

BÊLIT CRUMPLES BENEATH THE BLOW, LIKE A CHILD'S DOLL...

...AND KNOWS *NOTHING,* AS SHE IS CARRIED DOWN FROM THE PEAKS BY A *BRONZE-SKINNED* GIANT WHO MOVES AS SILENTLY AS A STALKING *LEOPARD.*

IT IS THE *FIRE'S* WARMTH THAT MAKES HER STIR, SOME TIME LATER...

...EVEN AS SHE SENSES THAT HER WRISTS ARE *BOUND.*

YOU ARE *AWAKE!* *GOOD!*

PERHAPS, YOU WERE *RIGHT,* WOMAN!

PERHAPS WE *WILL* TALK... JUST FOR *A LITTLE* WHILE!

I'LL *TALK* ALL RIGHT, YOU--

EPITHETS RISE UNBIDDEN, TO BÊLIT'S STILL-SMARTING MOUTH...

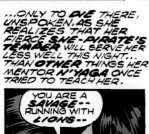

...ONLY TO *DIE* THERE, UNSPOKEN, AS SHE REALIZES THAT HER FIERCE *SHE-PIRATE'S TEMPER* WILL SERVE HER LESS WELL THIS NIGHT... THAN *OTHER* THINGS HER MENTOR *N'YAGA* ONCE TRIED TO TEACH HER.

YOU ARE A *SAVAGE--* RUNNING WITH *LIONS!*

--AND YOU SPEAK THE DIALECT OF THE *RIVER-FOLK,* SUCH AS THE *WATAMBIS!*

YET, THERE IS ANOTHER ACCENT *BENEATH* THAT ONE-- ONE I REMEMBER FROM *NYBORIAN* LANDS--!

YES! MY *FATHER* WAS OF SUCH A LAND--ONE CALLED *AK-LON-YA!*

YOU MUST MEAN-- *AQUILONIA!* IT IS THE *GREATEST* OF THE *NORTHERN LANDS!*

IT MEANS *NOTHING* TO ME BUT *ASHES* AND *MEMORIES...*

"YET, THEY ARE *SHARP* MEMORIES, OF A *SWIFT* JOURNEY BY HORSEBACK OVER *ROADLESS LANDS* --

"--THEN HURRIEDLY *OUT TO SEA* BY NIGHT, IN A BOAT WITH *MANY MEN!*

"I WAS BUT A *CHILD* THEN...

"...AND RECALL *LITTLE* OF MY FATHER, SAVE THAT HE HAD BEEN A *LORD* IN HIS NATIVE LAND...

"...AND THAT HE SAILED *SOUTH,* TO FLEE CERTAIN *ENEMIES* WITH *ROYAL-SOUNDING NAMES.*

"I REMEMBER BEING TOLD TO *HIDE,* WHEN THE CREW BATTLED *PIRATES* --

"--*BLOODTHIRSTY* MEN, FROM A PLACE HE CALLED THE *BARACHAN ISLES.*

"THEY WERE *DRIVEN OFF* --BUT WE THEN HAD *TOO FEW* MEN LEFT TO *MAN* THE BOAT --

"AND, WHEN A *STORM* STRUCK--A STORM WHOSE *FULL-MANED FURY* I CAN STILL FEEL, AFTER ALL THESE MANY *YEARS* --

"--ONLY MY *FATHER* AND I SURVIVED-- COLD AND WET, CLINGING TO WHAT LITTLE *REMAINED* OF THE VESSEL!

"MY FATHER WAS A *STRONG* MAN-- AND SOMEHOW, WE MADE IT TO THE SHORE *ALIVE.*"

"I SAW THERE THE *REMAINS* OF THOSE WHO DID *NOT.*"

"WE HEADED *NORTH* THEN..."

"PERHAPS MY FATHER HOPED TO FIND *CIVILIZATION,* AND A *NEW* SHIP."

"INSTEAD, HE FOUND ONLY *DEATH*-- AT *BLACK HANDS*--"

"--AND *I* WAS CARRIED OFF, *LIVING,* TOWARD AN END I COULD NOT *GUESS.*"

"BUT, THOSE GRIM WARRIORS WERE OF A TRIBE THAT WORSHIPS THE VELDT-- DWELLING *LION*..."

"AND, IN THEIR PATH, THEY SAW A LONE *LION CUB.*"

"TO KILL A LION-- *ANY* LION-- MEANT TO THEM THAT THE *SLAYER* WOULD GAIN A LION'S *COURAGE*..."

"THUS, THEY *SLEW* THE CUB-- AS FIERCELY AS THOUGH IT HAD BEEN A FULL-GROWN *KILLER!*"

"THEY THOUGH IT HAD STRAYED *FAR,* SINCE THE LION IS NOT BY NATURE A BEAST OF THE *JUNGLE*..."

"BUT, THESE WERE LIONS *UNLIKE* OTHERS-- LIONS WHICH PROWLED THE *FOREST* AS WELL AS THE *VELDT*--"

"--LIONS WHICH *CAME* AT THE CUB'S PITIFUL *DEATH-- SQUEAL*--"

"--LIONS WHICH *SLAUGHTERED* THE WARRIORS, LIKE SO MANY *CATTLE!*"

"THEN *I TOO* WOULD HAVE DIED, BUT FOR A GREAT TAWNY *FEMALE.*"

"IT WAS *HER* CUB THAT HAD BEEN SLAIN..."

"SHE WANTED THE *MANLING* TO TAKE ITS *PLACE*-- AND SHE WAS A FEMALE WHO *GOT* WHAT SHE WANTED!"

"THUS, I *SNARED* HER WITH HER CUB THAT STILL *LIVED*--AND WHOSE FUR WAS *DARK* AS THE SHROUDING *JUNGLE NIGHT.*

"I CALLED HIM *SHOLO,* WHICH MEANS *BLACK* IN THE RIVER DIALECT.

"IN TIME, I GREW TO *MANHOOD*--YET STILL, I RAN WITH THE *LION PRIDE*--

"AND *SHOLO,* SON OF SHOLO, RAN *WITH* ME--AS HAD HIS BLACK-MANED *FATHER.*

"SMALL *WONDER* THE DRAGON-RIDERS THINK ME A *WERE-BEAST!*

"WE PROWLED THE JUNGLE, EXPLORING *FARTHER INLAND* THAN EVER LIONS WENT BEFORE...

"...FOUND A *CITY* BUILT AND ABANDONED BY THE LION-WORSHIPPERS IN DAYS *THEY THEMSELVES* HAD FORGOTTEN.

"THERE WE BROUGHT THOSE OF THE TRIBE I COULD *CARRY AWAY ALIVE,* TO BE MY *SERVANTS...*

"...OR, IF THEY REFUSED, THE PRIDE'S NEXT *MEAL.*

"THEY CALLED ME *AMRA*--WHICH ONCE, AMONG THEIR PEOPLE, HAD MEANT '*FIRST AMONG LIONS*'!

"IT WAS A *WONDROUS* PLACE THIS LAIR OF LIONS--WHERE LONG-NEGLECTED *TREASURE* LAY, UNTOUCHED FOR *COUNTLESS MOONS.*

"FROM CHILDISH DAYS, I KNEW ITS *VALUE* IN THE *WORLD BEYOND.*

"TO *ME,* IT MEANT *NOTHING.*

"THERE WAS ALSO A *GREAT TOMB-LIKE WALL,* ON WHICH ARE *SIGNS* I CANNOT READ, NOR CAN *ANY* MAN NOW LIVING.

"I FEEL THEY HIDE A *MYSTERY.*

"PERHAPS *YOU* SHALL SOLVE IT FOR ME.

"AS FOR *YOURSELF*, YOU SHALL BECOME THE LATEST OF MY *BRIDES*--THOSE WOMEN WHOM THE DRAGON-RIDERS AND OTHERS SEND ME AS *TRIBUTE*, SO THAT I DO NOT SEND *SHOLO* AND THE *PRIDE* AGAINST THEM.

"THE LAST OF THE *MEN* HAVE FLED NOW, OR DIED--SO THE WOMEN LIVE FOR AS LONG AS THEY *AMUSE* ME, AND *SERVE* ME WELL.

"AS A RULE, THAT IS *NOT LONG*...

...BUT SINCE I HAVE *NEVER* IN MY YEARS OF MANHOOD SEEN A WOMAN OF *MY OWN KIND*...

...I SUSPECT THAT *YOU* WILL LAST *LONGER* THAN MOST!

YOU'LL *REGRET* HAULING ME OFF TO YOUR GOD-FORSAKEN CITY--THAT I *SWEAR*!

I AM *BÊLIT*--*BÊLIT*, DO YOU HEAR?

THE JUNGLE TRIBES REVERE ME AS A *GODDESS*!

EVEN IN THE JUNGLE FASTNESS, I HAVE HEARD THE LEGENDS OF *BÊLIT*, WHOSE NAME MEANS *GODDESS*!

WHO SHOULD MAKE A *BETTER* MATE FOR *AMRA*, THE LION?

AND MY MATE YOU *SHALL* BE--FOR AS LONG AS YOU *LIVE*!

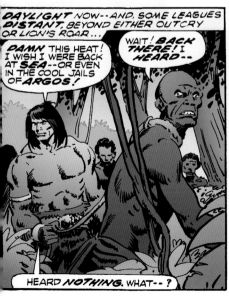

DAYLIGHT NOW--AND, SOME LEAGUES DISTANT, BEYOND EITHER OUTCRY OR LION'S ROAR...

DAMN THIS HEAT! I WISH I WERE BACK AT *SEA*--OR EVEN IN THE COOL JAILS OF *ARGOS*!

WAIT! *BACK THERE*! I *HEARD*--

HEARD *NOTHING*. WHAT--?

THIS SOUND, DOG!

THE SOUND OF MY FEET--*FLEEING*!

CURSE ME FOR A CLUMSY *FOOL*!

THIS JUNGLE ROBS ME OF MY *SHARPNESS*!

I WILL BRING HIM *DOWN*, WHITE-SKIN!

HOLD! DON'T *KILL* HIM!

WE WATAMBIS ARE *SKILLED WARRIORS,* WHITE-SKIN... NOT LIKE THOSE WHO TRUST TO *RIVER-DRAGONS!*

YOU *SEE?* I THREW THE SPEAR BUT TO *GRAZE* AND *FELL* HIM!

AGAIN I OWE YOU MY THANKS, ANAKI!

ON YOUR *FEET,* TINPAGA! THAT *SCRATCH* WASN'T ENOUGH TO --

CROM!!

A *BUSH-VIPER!*

IT *BIT* -- THAT DOG -- *KILLED* HIM!

WELL, IT WILL DO *NO MORE* KILLING --

BUT, THERE IS *UNCOMMON DEATH* IN THIS LAND WHERE *DAGON* IS CHIEFTAIN OF VILE GODS --

-- *DEATH* BENEATH EVERY *TREE-ROOT,* AND TAKING THE SHAPE OF EVERY *VINE!*

I'LL BE GLAD WHEN I'VE SEEN THE *LAST* OF KUSH AND LANDS SOUTH!

COME! THAT REPTILE-RIDING DOG DID US LITTLE GOOD, ANYWAY!

LET THE *JACKALS* BE HIS PALL-BEARERS!

WE WILL *YET* FIND SOME TRACK OF *BÊLIT,* BY DAY OR BY *NIGHT* --

"-- NO MATTER *WHERE* SHE HAS WANDERED IN HER FLIGHT!'"

LOOK, WOMAN OF THE SEA!

THERE IS A SIGHT YOU'VE NOT BEHELD FROM YOUR SHIP, EVEN BENEATH A ROUND-EYED *MOON...*

54

THE LAIR OF THE LIONS!

ISHTAR AND ASHTORETH! THAT GREAT STONE LION--ATOP THOSE GREAT PILLARS--!

CARVED BY THE HANDS OF SKILLED TRIBESMEN-- IN IN EXCHANGE FOR A FEW WEEKS MORE OF LIFE.

FOLLOW ME! THE WAY DOWN IS TREACHEROUS!

MINUTES LATER, THEY DRAW NEAR A CLEFT IN THE PARTLY-CRUMBLED WALL OF THE ANCIENT CITY...

...A CLEFT GUARDED BY GREAT CATS WHICH ROAR THEIR MISTRUST OF THE FEMALE AT THEIR LORD'S SIDE...

...ONLY TO GIVE WAY IN TURN TO A GREATER, EVEN MORE SAVAGE ROAR WHICH FREEZES BÊLIT'S BLOOD AS SURELY AS IF IT WERE UNEXPECTED...

...AND SENDS THE TAWNY BEASTS COWERING, AS MAN AND WOMAN AND BLACK-MANED LION PASS INTO THE CITY.

NOT FAR DISTANT, GIRL...

...IS MY TREASURE CHAMBER, OF WHICH I SPOKE BEFORE!

BY BEL, GOD OF ALL THIEVES--!

THIS IS A TREASURE-TROVE TO *SURPASS* ANY I KNOW FROM *KUSH* TO THE *BARACHAS!*

I'VE WAITED *LONG* TO SEE SO MUCH *RICHES* IN ONE PLACE--

THEN I'LL *BURY* YOU IN IT-- AND LET YOUR *BONES* WEAR THE *GOLD OF KINGS!*

WHAT? *WHO--?*

THAT, GIRL--

--IS *MAKEDA!*

SHE WAS A *PRINCESS* OF THE *FAR-OFF MOONHAWK TRIBE...*

...AND NOW IS *MISTRESS OF THE LAIR OF THE LIONS!*

IS THAT NOT *SO,* MY *AMRA?*

DID YOU *TELL* YOUR NEW PET THAT I HAVE *OUTLIVED* MANY A WENCH WHO SOUGHT TO *REPLACE* ME IN YOUR *AFFECTIONS--*

-- AND THAT THOSE I COULD NOT *WOO* YOU FROM, I *SLEW*-- WITH MY *BARE HANDS!?*

YOU TELL *QUITE A STORY* ONE OUTBURST, MAKEDA!

BUT THOSE WERE DOUBTLESS *TERRIFIED, FRAGILE MAIDENS* YOU SLEW--

--WHILE I AM *BÊLIT--*

OOOOFFF

--QUEEN OF THE BLACK COAST!

I'LL MAKE YOU *QUEEN OF SHADES,* YOU PALE-SKINNED *WITCH!*

THIS CLAW IS AS DEADLY AS ANY *LION'S!*

A CLAW YOU'LL *NOT* USE IT ON *THIS* ONE!

SO SPEAKS *AMRA!*

LET ME GO! I--

I *WILL* LET YOU GO, MAKEDA-- BECAUSE YOU *PLEASED* ME MORE THAN MOST, WITH YOUR VERY *FIERCENESS!*

BUT *GO--* AND GO *QUICKLY,* AND NEVER *RETURN* TO THIS *LAIR OF LIONS--*

--OR I WILL *RELEASE* YOU FROM MY PROTECTION, AND YOU'LL MAKE A *MORSEL* FOR MY *GREAT CATS!*

I-WILL *GO--* MY AMRA--!

THE MOON IS STILL *HIGH* AS THE DETHRONED DEMI-QUEEN STALKS INTO THE SURROUNDING JUNGLE.

FULL OF HURT AND ANGER, SHE FORGETS FOR A FLEETING MOMENT...

...THAT LIONS ARE NOT THE ONLY PREDATORS THAT STALK THE NIGHT!

OHHHH--!

AMRA!

AMRA--!

YET, IT IS NOT *AMRA* WHO SEES THE HURTLING *LEOPARD*--

--BUT ANOTHER, LIKEWISE MADE OF STEEL AND SINEW!

UNPREPARED FOR THE ATTACK FROM ANOTHER QUARTER, THE SPOTTED CAT WRITHES AND FLAILS IN THE GRIP OF THOSE MIGHTY, EVER-TIGHTENING ARMS--

--TILL A SINGLE, UNMISTAKABLE CRACK IS HEARD --

--AND ONLY ONE PRIMEVAL FIGURE RISES, WHERE TWO WENT DOWN!

CROM TAKE ME-- *MORE* DEATH!

IS THERE NEVER--AN *END* TO IT--?

AIEEE! IS THIS SOME DEVILTRY OF THE *TRICKSTER GOD* ?

ANOTHER *WHITE-SKIN*-- LIKE *AMRA*-- LIKE THE *WENCH*--!

WENCH?

I DON'T KNOW WHO YOU *ARE*, GIRL --

BUT, BY CROM, YOU'RE GOING TO *TAKE* ME TO THIS WENCH, AND TO THIS *AMRA*!

--*RIGHT NOW*, DO YOU *HEAR* ME??

YES-- *YES,* I WILL DO AS YOU *SAY*--

HOWEVER, YOU WILL *NEVER* ARRIVE--IN TIME TO *SAVE* THEM. IF SAVE THEM YOU *COULD!*

WHAT DO YOU *MEAN,* WOMAN?

AMRA *CAST ME OUT* THIS NIGHT!

--ME, *MAKEDA*--

"YET, A *DAUGHTER OF MANY WARRIOR-KINGS* DOES NOT GO *MEEKLY* INTO THE DARKLING NIGHT!"

"*FIRST,* TORCH IN HAND, I *DESCENDED* UNDER AMRA'S BLEAK CITY..."

...TO STAND BEFORE THE *ANCIENT TOMB-WALL,* WHERE NAMELESS WRITINGS ARE CARVED WHICH *NONE* HAVE BEEN KNOWN TO DECIPHER.

"BUT, I KNOW *MORE* THAN OTHERS--AND LEARNED, WITHOUT AMRA'S KNOWLEDGE, TO *READ* THEM!"

"THEY ARE *SPELLS*-- SPELLS THAT *BIND!*"

"AND, BY MEANS OF *OTHER* SPELLS, WHICH I ALONE COULD *READ* IN THE TORCH'S GLARE..."

"...THOSE WHO *HAVE* BEEN LONG BOUND..."

...ARE NOW *UNLEASHED!*

YOUR WOMAN IS *DOOMED,* WHITE-SKIN--

DOOMED!

AND, AT THAT VERY INSTANT--SOMEWHERE IN THE DEEP MURKY BLACKNESS *FAR BENEATH* THE LAIR OF THE LIONS--

--TALONED HANDS STIR!

THIS WILL BE THE BLOOD-MOONED NIGHT THEY HAVE AWAITED FOR A THOUSAND UPON A THOUSAND YEARS!

NEXT ISSUE: **CONAN** VS. **AMRA**... **TO THE DEATH!**

"Know, O prince, that between the years when the oceans drank Atlantis and the gleaming cities, and the rise of the sons of Aryas, there was an Age undreamed of, when shining kingdoms lay spread across the world like blue mantles beneath the stars. "Hither came Conan, the Cimmerian, black-haired, sullen-eyed, sword in hand, a thief, a reaver, a slayer, with gigantic melancholies and gigantic mirth, to tread the jeweled thrones of the Earth under his sandaled feet."

—The Nemedian Chronicles.

I DON'T LIKE THE LOOK OF THE PLACE ANY MORE THAN *YOU* DO, ANAKI!

BUT, THAT DEVIL CALLED *AMRA*, WHOEVER HE IS, CARRIED OFF MY WOMAN *BÉLIT*--OR AT LEAST, SO THIS *CAST-OFF WENCH* SAYS!

I AM *NO* CAST-OFF...BUT THE DAUGHTER OF *WARRIOR-KINGS*, AND ONCE THE BRIDE OF AMRA *MYSELF!*

MAYBE *SO*-- BUT THAT DIDN'T STOP HIM FROM SEEKING *ANOTHER*, DID IT?

BUT, NEVER MIND-- YOU CAN HAVE HIM *BACK*, IF HE'LL SURRENDER HER *PEACEFULLY*, AND--

CROM! WHAT'S *THAT??*

IT IS-- *AMRA*--

--AYE, *AMRA* HIMSELF-- AND HE LEADS HIS *NEW* BRIDE TO THE *LION-ALTAR!*

IT IS THERE THAT THE *WEDDING RITES* ARE ALWAYS PERFORMED-- WITH THE *GREAT CATS* THEIR ONLY WITNESS!

WEDDING? THERE'LL BE *NO* WEDDING OR ANYTHING *ELSE* TONIGHT--

I *SWEAR* IT, BY ALL THE GODS FROM *CIMMERIA* TO *KUSH!*

NO, THERE'LL *NOT* BE, MAKEDA THINKS --BUT FOR REASONS THE WHITE-SKIN HAS CHOSEN TO *IGNORE*--

MAKEDA THINKS BACK ON HOW HER BELOVED AMRA *EXPELLED* HER FROM HIS DESERTED CITY-- AND ALL FOR THE SAKE OF THAT *ACCURSED BÉLIT*--

BUT, SHE'LL HAVE HER *REVENGE*--FOR, MAKEDA ALONE COULD READ THE *INSCRIPTIONS* ON THE ANCIENT *TOMBS* BENEATH THE RUINS--

--*SPELLS* WHICH, SHORTLY BEFORE, BROUGHT FORTH *SHADOWY HORRORS* WHICH SHE FLED, *UNSEEING!*

THEY ARE STILL *DOWN* THERE-- THIS SHE *KNOWS!*

WELL? WHAT ARE YOU *WAITING* FOR, WOMAN?

IF YOU VALUE YOUR HIDE, YOU'LL SHOW ME THE *FASTEST PATH* TO THAT ALTAR!

I SHALL... BUT YOU'LL NOT *LIVE* LONG AFTER *REGRETTING* IT!

WE'LL *SEE!*

COME, YOU WATAMBIS! IF YOU HANG BACK FOR FEAR OF AMRA--

--THEN PRESS FORWARD NOW, FOR FEAR OF ME!

WE COME, WHITE-SKIN!

ANAKI...DO YOU THINK EVEN THE MATE OF BÊLIT CAN STAND AGAINST THE FABLED AMRA?

I DO NOT KNOW! BUT WE SHALL, AND SOONER THAN WE WILL!

CONAN HEARS THE FURTIVE WHISPERS, BUT SAYS NOTHING...

...PERHAPS BECAUSE, DEEP IN HIS BARBARIAN'S HEART, HE HIMSELF WONDERS HOW HE WILL FARE IF IT COMES TO BATTLE WITH A MAN WHO RUNS WITH RAGING LIONS.

INSTEAD, HE QUICKENS HIS STEP...

...AS, DIMLY, HE HEARS SCANT SNATCHES OF THE LOVE-CHANT OF THIS SON OF AN AQUILONIAN NOBLE, REARED TO SAVAGERY BY FANGED KILLERS--

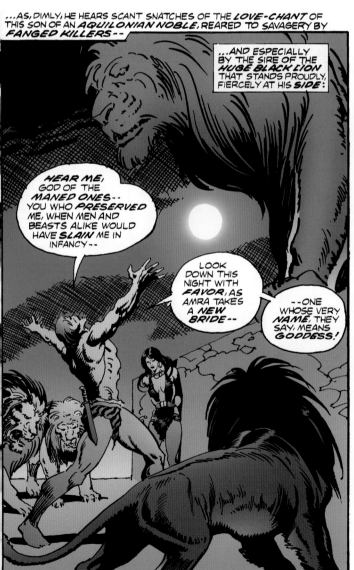

...AND ESPECIALLY BY THE SIRE OF THE HUGE BLACK LION THAT STANDS PROUDLY, FIERCELY AT HIS SIDE:

HEAR ME, GOD OF THE MANED ONES-- YOU WHO PRESERVED ME, WHEN MEN AND BEASTS ALIKE WOULD HAVE SLAIN ME IN INFANCY--

LOOK DOWN THIS NIGHT WITH FAVOR, AS AMRA TAKES A NEW BRIDE--

--ONE WHOSE VERY NAME, THEY SAY, MEANS GODDESS!

YOU SPEAK HUMAN WORDS--YET ALWAYS, THE SNARL OF THE WILD ANIMAL LIES JUST BENEATH THE SURFACE!

IF YOU WERE HUMAN, YOU WOULD HEED ME WHEN I SAY I ALREADY HAVE A MATE--

--ONE WHO WILL CUT YOU TO RIBBONS IF YOU DON'T-- :ARRRH!: YOU FILTHY JACKAL--!

JACKAL!? I SHOULD FEED YOU TO MY LIONS FOR CALLING ME THAT!

YOU ARE *AMRA'S* NOW-- AND YOUR MATE WILL *DIE* IF HE TRIES TO CLAIM YOU!

SO, YOU ARE *QUIET* NOW! *GOOD!*

BUT, THERE IS *REASON* FOR THE SHE-PIRATE'S SUDDEN SILENCE...

...AS, UNKNOWN TO HER *EERIE* CAPTOR, SHE WORKS HER *WRIST-BONDS* MORE WILDLY THAN EVER-- TILL A *TRACE OF BLOOD* TRICKLES DOWN--

- TO *DRIVE MAD* ONE OF THE *YOUNGER LIONS* THERE BENEATH THE WIDE-EYED MOON!

RRARR

RRARK

AMRA'S ANSWERING ROAR IS EVEN MORE *BESTIAL* THAN THE LION'S--

--HIS *LEAP* EVEN *SWIFTER*--!

NO MAN IS STRONGER THAN A LION-- AND THOSE WHO SAY OTHERWISE ARE FULL OF *BAD WINE* OR *WORSE LIES.*

GRARY

YET, SINCE *CHILDHOOD,* AMRA HAS *KNOWN* THE WAYS OF THE TAWNY CATS--

HE CAN *SENSE* THEIR COMING MOVES--

--*EVADE* THEIR RAKING TALONS--

--WHILE HIS OWN *KNIFE* BITES DEEP *AGAIN*--

--AND *AGAIN*--

-- IN A *MURDEROUS BLUR* WHICH EVEN BELIT'S HAWK-EYES CANNOT FOLLOW--

RNK!

--TILL IT SUDDENLY SEVERS THE *RENEGADE BEAST'S JUGULAR!*

THEN, ONCE MORE, THE **ROAR OF THE LION-LORD** IS HEARD IN THE LAND--

--A ROAR EVEN MORE **FRIGHTENING** THAN THAT OF THE HUGE **CARNIVORES** THEMSELVES--

--AND NO MORE **HUMAN!**

THEN, THE MOMENT **FADES**--AND HE IS A **MAN** ONCE MORE.

FOR THE MOMENT.

NOW DO YOU SEE, WOMAN?

NOW DO YOU SEE WHY **NO ONE** CAN TAKE YOU **FROM** ME?

I AM **AMRA!**

AMRA!!

I AM **KING** HERE--AND **NONE** CAN EVER **DEFY** ME!

BÊLIT LOOKS ON, AND SAYS **NOTHING**...

BUT SHE, TOO, WONDERS IF EVEN HER **BARBARIAN LOVER** FROM OUT OF THE FIERCE **NORTHLAND** COULD STAND AGAINST THIS SCION OF **JUNGLE** AND **JUJU**...!

THEY MOVE **WITHOUT SOUND** THRU THE NIGHT, THESE WATAMBIS--LIKE THE TRAINED **WARRIORS** THEY ARE--COMING SWIFTLY TO THE ONE GREAT **CLEFT** IN THE RUINED CITY'S WALL.

THEN, WITHOUT HESITATION YET SILENTLY AS A **PANTHER**, THEIR GRIM LEADER GLIDES **THRU** THE GAPING APERTURE...

...TO COME FACE TO FACE WITH THE LONG-MANED SPECTRE OF **DEATH!**

CROM!

GRRR

63

THE LION WAS LEFT TO *GUARD* THE ENTRANCE-WAY...AND TO HIM, THE COMMAND OF *AMRA* IS A *LIVING LAW.*

BUT, THIS MAN IS NOT LIKE THE *OTHERS* HIS CLAWS HAVE RAKED AND RAVAGED...

RRRR

THIS IS *CONAN, THE CIMMERIAN...*

...WHO HAS FOUGHT THE *DEMONS* OF THE AIR, AND THE *DEVILS* OF THE DEEP PLACES!

HE HAS TIME ONLY FOR ONE THRUSTING *SWORD-STROKE...*

BUT, IT IS A *SURE* ONE.

WE'RE...*LUCKY!* IF THERE HAD BEEN *TWO* OF THESE THINGS...!

...*YOU* WOULD HAVE MADE A MEAL FOR THE *VULTURES!*

YOU ARE AN EVEN *MIGHTIER* WARRIOR THAN I HAD IMAGINED...

...THOUGH *AMRA* COULD HAVE SLAIN THAT BEAST WITH NAUGHT BUT A *KNIFE!*

STILL, PERHAPS YOU *WILL* SLAY HIM--AND WIN MY *REVENGE* FOR ME!

TO *SEVEN HELLS* WITH YOUR BLOODLUST, WOMAN I CAME FOR MY *MATE*--AND NOTHING *MORE!*

AND YOU MAY *HAVE* HER...

...BUT ONLY OVER *AMRA'S* *LIFELESS BODY!*

WHILE, *ABOVE,* NEAR THE TOWERING *ALTAR...*

DID YOU *HEAR,* SHOLO? AN *INTRUDER* HAS COME INTO THE LAIR OF LIONS!

RAWR

WHETHER MAN OR BRUTE, HE'LL NOT *LIVE* TO-- *WHAT--?*

AMRA!

WHAT IN *ISHTAR'S* NAME--?

THE *STONE* FALLS AWAY-- BENEATH THE *WOMAN*--!

SHE IS GONE!

BUT WHERE? WHO WOULD HAVE DARED--?

AN INSTANT LATER, ALL QUERIES FREEZE ON THE LION-MAN'S LIPS...

...AS, FROM THE DANK BLACKNESS BELOW, A SLAVERING AND MURKY HORDE SPEWS FORTH...!

GOD OF THE MANED ONES!

AMRA SPEAKS NO MORE--

--BUT LASHES OUT AT THE SIX-LIMBED, SPIDERY GNOMES--

--AND SNARLS WITH PLEASURE TO LEARN, AT LEAST, THAT THEY ARE FLESH AND BLOOD!

YET, IF THEY ARE MORTAL, THEY ARE ALSO AS MANY, IT SEEMS, AS THE TREES IN THE SPRAWLING JUNGLE...

AND, SO HUNGRY ARE THEY FOR HUMAN FLESH WHICH HAS BEEN DENIED THEM FOR A THOUSAND CENTURIES...

...THAT THEY KNOW NO FEAR, NOT EVEN OF THE GREAT BLACK LION AND HIS TALONED PRIDE!

STILL, THEY SWIFTLY FIND, EVEN AS THEY CLAMBER OVER DARK AND TAWNY FORMS, THAT LIONS, TOO, HAVE A SIMPLE CREDO:

WHAT CAN BE CLAWED OR BITTEN...CAN BE KILLED!

MEANWHILE, AMRA HAS CUT HIS WAY FREE, AND--

HO, SHOLO! HO, YOU GREAT CATS!

FOLLOW YOUR BROTHER--TO RECOVER HIS CHOSEN MATE!

AS, FAR BELOW...

WHAT'S ALL THAT *UPROAR,* ABOVE US?

IT MUST BE--THOSE WHO I *LOOSED* FROM THEIR AGE-OLD *SPELL!*

WE MUST *TURN BACK!* I AM *AFRAID...!*

WE'LL TURN BACK WHEN *BÊLIT* IS BY MY SIDE, AND NOT *BEFORE!*

NOW, *WHICH WAY?*

TH-THRU *HERE--!*

THIS *PASSAGE* LEADS DIRECTLY BENEATH THE *LION-ALTAR,* AND THEN--

AND THEN *WE'LL DO THE REST!*

BUT-- WHAT'S THAT *SCRAPING* SOUND?

THE *UNBOUND ONES!* AIEEEEEE--!

CROM'S DEVILS!

VOICELESS THEY ARE...

NOR, IN TRUTH, HAVE THEY HAD MUCH TO *TALK* ABOUT IN COUNTLESS AGES OF UNRELIEVED *DARKNESS...*

ONLY THEIR *CLAWED HANDS* AND RAZOR-SHARP *FANGS* SPEAK FOR THEM...

AND THESE ARE DULY *ANSWERED,* BY A BROADSWORD FORGED OF HARD *NYRMANIAN STEEL!*

BACK, YOU *HELLSPAWN!* BACK!

YOU CAN *HAVE* HIS WOMAN, FOR ALL I *CARE--* AND FOR WHATEVER *PURPOSE--*

--BUT *NOT* TILL SHE'S LED ME TO THE *ONE* I SEEK!

TILL THEN-- GIVE WAY, OR *DIE!*

AND DIE THEY **DO**--FOR, IT WAS ONLY A SMALL **OFF-BRANCHING** OF THE FOUR ARMED HORDE, AFTER ALL.

YET, THEY DO NOT GO **ALONE** TO THEIR HOUSE OF SHADES...

THERE'LL BE **WEEPING** AND **WAILING** FOR THIS LOST BROTHER, WHEN-- AND **IF**--HIS FELLOW WATAMBIS RETURN TO THEIR FAR-OFF VILLAGE.

BUT, FOR **NOW**--

LET'S **GO**....!

SKELETONS! YOUR LORD AND MASTER IS A **CRUEL** MAN, MAKEDA!

ONE CANNOT INSTILL **FEAR** IN HUMAN HEARTS UNLESS ONE IS **MERCILESS**, WHITE-SKIN!

THESE MEN WERE **NOTHING**!

A **CURIOUS** JUDGMENT -- SINCE HE SENT **YOU** FORTH INTO THE JUNGLE TO DIE, AS WELL...

...AND SINCE YOU UNLEASHED THOSE **DEMON-DWARVES** TO GAIN **REVENGE** ON HIM!

AT HIS OWN MENTION OF THE DWELLERS IN DARKNESS, CONAN GROWS GRIMLY **SILENT** ONCE MORE...

FOR, HE KNOWS THAT THERE ARE **FAR MORE** OF THEM, IN THE SURROUNDING **WALLS**--AND BENEATH THEIR VERY **FEET**--

FOR A FLEETING MOMENT, HE **THINKS BACK** ON ALL THE LOATHSOME, TIME-FORGOTTEN **HORRORS** HE'S BATTLED IN HIS NIGH SCORE OF YEARS-- AND HOW **MANY** OF THEM WERE BIRTHED BY THE FEARSOME **EARTH-MOTHER** HERSELF--

AND, HIS **BARBARIAN MIND** SHUDDERS AT THE KNOWLEDGE OF HOW MANY **OTHER** NAMELESS TERRORS MUST LIE SLEEPING THERE, JUST OUT OF SIGHT OF AN UNSUSPECTING **HUMANKIND**.

BUT, EVEN AN *INSTANT'S* REVERIE IS SUDDENLY *SLASHED TO RIBBONS* BY--

AIEEE!

BÈLIT!

WHERE ARE YOU??

OVER HERE, CONAN--HURRY!

IN THE NAME OF ISHTAR-- HURRY!

FROM THE DEPTHS *BELOW* THIS NETHERMOST LEVEL OF THE RUINS, THERE IS TRULY *NO RETURN*...

...AND *TWO MEN* HAVE RACED HITHER, TO SAVE THE *SOUL* AND *BODY* OF THE SHEMITISH *SHE-PIRATE* WHOM BOTH LOVE IN THEIR SEPARATE, SAVAGE *WAYS*--!

AND *NO* MAN COULD SAY WITH CERTAINTY--NAY, NOT EVEN ONE OF THE SELF-ASSURED *NEMEDIAN SCHOLARS*--

--WHETHER THE LONG *BROADSWORD* OF THE BLOODMAD *BARBARIAN*--

--BITES DEEPER OR MORE DEADLY THAN THE SHARP BLADE OF THE VENGEFUL *JUNGLE LORD*!

WHAT *MATTERS* IS THAT, BETWEEN THEM -- AND *WITHOUT A WORD* -- THEY LAY LOW LAYER UPON *LAYER* OF MISSHAPEN GARGOYLES --

-- AT LENGTH FIGHTING *BACK TO BACK*, EACH AS AWARE OF THE OTHER'S PRESENCE AS IF HE FOUGHT WITH A POISONOUS *VIPER* AT HIS HEEL --

-- YET WITH THEIR *CONFLICTING* PASSIONS *BURIED* IN THE HEAT OF THE MOMENT!

NOR IS IT ANY SHELTERED *HYBORIAN LADY* FOR WHOM THESE TWO GIANTS DO FRENZIED BATTLE...

-- BUT *BÊLIT*, SELF-CROWNED QUEEN OF THE BLACK COAST!

GIVE SUCH A ONE BUT A *JAGGED STONE*, SHARP ENOUGH TO CUT HER OWN *BONDS* --

-- AND SHE CAN TAKE CARE OF *HERSELF!*

SHE IS *ANGERED* THAT SHE HAS BEEN TREATED SO CONTEMPTUOUSLY BY THE *LION-LORD*, AS *PROPERTY* TO BE DISPOSED OF RATHER THAN AS A *WARRIOR* IN HER OWN RIGHT...

BUT SUCH THOUGHTS CAN WAIT FOR *LATER.*

RIGHT NOW, THE SPIDER-THINGS HAVE *THREE* NORTH-BORN WHIRLWINDS TO CONTEND WITH --

-- THE *WOMAN* FIGHTING AS FIERCELY AS EITHER *MAN!*

AND THE **WATAMBIS**, THOUGH THEY JOURNEYED FORTH TO STRIVE MAINLY WITH NOW-DEAD **DRAGON RIDERS**...

...PUT THEIR **SPEARS** TO DEADLY USE AGAINST **EARTHSPAWN** AS WELL!

THEN, WITHOUT WARNING, THE CLAMBERING DARK-DWELLERS SEEM TO **ADMIT DEFEAT**...

...AND, STILL SILENT AS THE **PLAGUE** WHICH KILLS, FLEE BACK TO THEIR UNCHARTED **DEPTHS**...

...WHICH **NONE** CAN IMAGINE, WHO HAS EVER LOOKED UPON THE **LIGHT OF DAY.**

BUT, THEY HAVE LEFT BEHIND **ONE** CASUALTY PREVIOUSLY **UNNOTICED**...

MAKEDA--DEAD! SHE WAS A **VENGEFUL** WENCH, YET SHE **LOVED**, IN HER STRANGE WAY!

LOVED **YOU**, LORD OF LIONS!

SHE WAS... **NOTHING** TO ME!

ONE CANNOT LIVE WITH **YESTERDAY'S MATE!**

NOW **STAND ASIDE**, MAN OF THE **OUTLANDS**--FOR **THIS** WOMAN BELONGS TO **AMRA!**

I BELONG TO **NO** MAN--BUT **THIS** MAN IS MY **CHOSEN** MATE!

I HAVE **NO QUARREL** WITH YOU, AMRA...

LET US PART IN **PEACE**--AS **WARRIORS** WHO HAVE FOUGHT A HIDEOUS FOE, SIDE BY SIDE!

NO! SHE IS **AMRA'S,** I SAY--IF I MUST **KILL** FOR HER!

THEN YOU **MUST** KILL--OR ELSE **BE** KILLED!

HE IS A **WILD BEAST**, MY BARBARIAN--WITH A **LION'S** WAYS--!

AND I AM A **MAN**, WHO HAS **SLAIN** LIONS, IN HIS DAY!

ANAKI! YOUR **KNIFE**--THAT WE MAY BE EVENLY MATCHED!

HE HAS **NO** LIONS DOWN HERE TO CARRY OUT HIS COMMANDS...

70

NOW, WE'LL SEE HOW HE FARES *WITHOUT* THEM!

NAMELESS *HYENA!* I NEED *NO* OTHERS TO DO BATTLE FOR ME!

FOR LONG YEARS, THE NAME OF *AMRA* HAS BEEN A *LEGEND ALIVE* IN THIS LAND--

--AND THE *LAST* THING YOU SHALL LEARN BEFORE YOU DIE--

--IS *WHY!*

THE LION-MAN, HOWEVER, THOUGH SWIFT AS THOSE HE LEADS, IS USED TO *LESSER* HUMAN FOES--

-- AND FAR *SLOWER* ONES!

STILL, IT TAKES BUT A *MOMENT* FOR HIM TO JUDGE *ANEW* THIS GRIM ENEMY...

...AND TO *RISE*, BEFORE THE BLACK-MANED BARBARIAN COULD POSSIBLY TAKE *ADVANTAGE* OF HIS FALLEN STATE!

RARR

ARRRR

AS FOR *BÊLIT*-- SHE WANTS *CONAN* TO WIN-- DESIRES IT WITH ALL HER *HEART*--

YET, AS THE TWO MEN COME TOGETHER LIKE TWO *RAGING BEASTS,* SHE FINDS IT HARD FOR AN INSTANT TO REMEMBER *WHICH* OF THEM HAS WANDERED FOR YEARS AMONG THE *HYBORIAN KINGDOMS*--

--AND WHICH WAS RAISED BY *WILD ANIMALS!*

71

LIKE TWO *TITANS* FROM BEYOND THE FRINGE OF TIME, THEY *MEET*--WRIST STRAINING AGAINST WRIST, AND SOUL AGAINST SOUL--

SAVAGE EYES MEET BRIEFLY-- AND PERHAPS, IN THAT SWIFT-PASSING INSTANT, THESE TWO STAR-CROSSED STRANGERS FINALLY *KNOW* EACH OTHER--

--KNOW THAT THEY WERE *BORN* AND GREW TO *MANHOOD* ALL IN UNKNOWN PREPARATION FOR THIS *MOMENT OF TRUTH!*

THEN, AFTER A SEEMING *ETERNITY* OF TENSE MOTIONLESSNESS, THE KNIFE-HAND OF THE *LION-LORD* BEGINS TO MOVE ITS SHARP BLADE *CLOSER* TO ITS GOAL--

--A PRECIOUS *INCH* AT A TIME--

--UNTIL IT IS *HALTED* BY A GARGANTUAN SURGE OF CIMMERIAN *WILL*, ONLY A HAIR'S BREADTH FROM BRONZED FLESH!

THEN, SUMMONING STRENGTH FROM SOME HIDDEN, INNER *WELL*, THE BARBARIAN MOVES THAT HAND SLOWLY, SLOWLY *BACK*--

--TILL THESE MEN SEEM AGAIN A PAIR OF MARBLE *STATUES*, CARVED BY THE FINEST ARTISANS OF *AQUILONIA*--

--OR ELSE TWIN FIGURES CARVED FROM A *GLACIER* IN THE FROZEN NORTHLAND WHERE CONAN FIRST ROAMED.

THEN, WITH A CAT'S SWIFTNESS--

--IT IS *AMRA* WHO BREAKS THE GRIM TABLEAU--

--AND SENDS *BOTH MEN* SPRAWLING TO THE COLD STONE FLOOR--

--*HIMSELF* ON TOP!

THEY *STRUGGLE* THERE, KNIVES FLASHING DARKLY IN AND OUT OF VIEW--

--WHILE *WATAMBIS* AND *WARRIOR WOMAN* WATCH--

--AS *MESMERIZED* AS EVER AN ARISTOCRATIC *VENDHYAN* WAS BY A SWAYING *COBRA.*

UNSEEN BY THEM IN THE BLACKNESS, CONAN'S *EYES* BLAZED WITH BLUE-FIRE *FURY*--

--WHILE AMRA *SNARLS*, HIS TEETH GNASHING IN A *MAN-KILLER'S RAGE!*

THEN, OF A *SUDDEN*-- THE LION-LORD'S HAND *PULLS BACK* ITS THRUSTING METAL BLADE--

--EVEN AS CONAN'S HAND *FALL AWAY,* SPENT--

--AND NO *TRUMPET CALL* COULD SOUND MORE CLEARLY--

--THAT THE FIGHT IS *ENDED.*

CONAN--?

73

AND THEN, THE WIDE-EYED AMRA *TURNS* SLIGHTLY IN THE SHIMMERING HALF-LIGHT...

...TO *FALL*, PUSHED ASIDE BY THE HAND OF *HIM WHO LIVES!*

CONAN! PRAISE BE TO *ISHTAR!*

FOR A MOMENT, THE DANK HALL IS FILLED TO OVERFLOWING WITH THE *TRIUMPHAL SHOUTS* OF THE TWO REMAINING *WATAMBIS...*

SILENCE, ANAKI-- OTARI!

IT WAS A *BRAVE* MAN I SLEW HERE.

IF WE'D MET *ANOTHER* DAY, WE MIGHT HAVE BEEN --*FRIENDS!*

I'M JUST GLAD IT'S *HE* THAT DIED-- AND NOT *YOU*, MY BARBARIAN!

WE ARE *SAFE* AT LAST--*ALL* OF US--

--AND THERE IS MUCH *TREASURE* HERE FOR THE *TAK*--

WHAT THE *DEVIL*--?

BY THE BONES OF *CROM!*

THE WHOLE PLACE IS *SHAKING*-- CRUMBLING DOWN *AROUND* US--!

RUN, DAMN YOUR HIDES--

RUN!!

LIKE SURE-FOOTED *WOLVES*, THE FOUR INTRUDERS FLEE BACK *OUT* OF THE SUNKEN TOMB--

--AND THRU THE YAWNING *CREVICE*, AN INSTANT BEFORE IT TUMBLES INTO *FINAL RUIN* BEHIND THEM.

THE *REMAINDER* OF THE VAST ONCE-CITY, WHICH HAS DEFIED THE RAVAGES OF *TIME* AND THE CREEPING *JUNGLE* FOR A THOUSAND UPON A THOUSAND YEARS, NOW *LIKEWISE* TOPPLES INTO WRECK AND RUIN--

--TILL SCARCELY A *STONE* IS LEFT ATOP A STONE IT *KNEW*--

--WHILE SNARLING, *TAWNY SHAPES* LOPE, *LEADERLESS* NOW BY MAN AND BEAST, FOR THE *SECURITY* OF THE WAITING RAIN-FOREST.

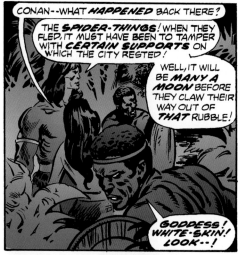

CONAN--WHAT *HAPPENED* BACK THERE?

THE *SPIDER-THINGS!* WHEN THEY FLED, IT MUST HAVE BEEN TO TAMPER WITH *CERTAIN SUPPORTS* ON WHICH THE CITY RESTED!

WELL, IT WILL BE *MANY A MOON* BEFORE THEY CLAW THEIR WAY OUT OF *THAT* RUBBLE!

GODDESS! WHITE-SKIN! LOOK--!

THE BLACK LION!

WITHOUT A SOUND OF ANY KIND, THE HUGE *CARNIVORE* PADS STRAIGHT TOWARD THE TENSE, UNMOVING FOURSOME.

THEN, KNOWING FLIGHT TO BE *FUTILE*, THE DARK-MANED BARBARIAN MOVES SUDDENLY TO THE *FORE*...

GET BACK, WOMAN!

MY SWORD'S *BURIED* BACK THERE-- AND MY KNIFE MAY NOT BE ENOUGH TO *SLAY* THAT BLACK DEVIL--

--BUT I SWEAR I'LL *MINGLE* HIS BLOOD WITH HIS *MASTER'S* ON IT, BEFORE I DIE!

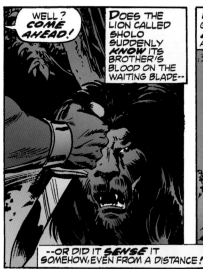

WELL? COME AHEAD!

DOES THE LION CALLED *SHOLO* SUDDENLY *KNOW* ITS BROTHER'S BLOOD ON THE WAITING BLADE--

--OR DID IT *SENSE* IT SOMEHOW, EVEN FROM A DISTANCE!

WHATEVER THE TRUTH, THE GREAT BEAST *HALTS* NOW--AND *LOWERS ITS HEAD*, AS IF TO ACKNOWLEDGE A *NEW* LORD OF LIONS --

--THEN SHAKES ITS JET-BLACK MANE AND *ROARS* ITS NEWFOUND ALLEGIANCE TO THE SHROUDING *NIGHT*.

NEXT, IT *TURNS AWAY* WITHOUT A BACK-WARD GLANCE AT THE POISED KNIFE-- TO *VANISH* INTO THE SURROUNDING JUNGLE.

CROM AND MITRA! I'M NOT SURE I KNOW WHAT *HAPPENED* JUST THEN--

--BUT I'M GLAD IT *DID!*

IT IS *TOLD*, WHITE-SKIN, THAT THERE SHALL *ALWAYS* BE AN *AMRA* --A *FIRST AMONG LIONS!*

--AND THE BLACK LION *KNEW* IT!

IF ONE IS DEAD, THEN *YOU* ARE NOW HE--

DID YOU *HEAR*, MY LOVER? YOU *ARE* AMRA NOW--AND THE *JUNGLE DRUMS* SHALL SPEAK OF YOU--

--AND ALL SHALL *FEAR*, EVEN MORE THAN *BEFORE!*

WELL--I GUESS IF YOU CAN BE A *GODDESS*, WOMAN--

--IT'S NOT TOO MUCH FOR *ME* TO BE-- A LION!

NOW, LET'S GET *MOVING!*

"IT'S A *LONG WAY* BACK TO THE *BLACK COAST!*"

END

76

"Know, O prince, that between the years when the oceans drank Atlantis and the gleaming cities, and the rise of the sons of Aryas, there was an Age undreamed of, when shining kingdoms lay spread across the world like blue mantles beneath the stars.

"Hither came Conan, the Cimmerian, black-haired, sullen-eyed, sword in hand, a thief, a reaver, a slayer, with gigantic melancholies and gigantic mirth, to tread the jeweled thrones of the Earth under his sandaled feet."

—The Nemedian Chronicles.

STAN LEE PRESENTS: CONAN THE BARBARIAN™

FIENDS OF THE FEATHERED SERPENT!

HE IS AMRA NOW-- AMRA THE LION!

ALONG THE BLACK COAST, THE JUNGLE TOM-TOMS BEAT IN THE NIGHT, WITH A TALE THAT THE SHE-DEVIL OF THE SEA HAS FOUND A MATE--

--A MAN OF IRON, WHOSE WRATH IS THAT OF A WOUNDED LION!

A VOYAGE INTO WEIRD WORLDS OF WONDER BY:
ROY THOMAS & JOHN BUSCEMA
WRITER/EDITOR   ARTIST

THE TRIBE EMBELLISHERS

JOE ROSEN, LETTERER

JV353

FREELY ADAPTED FROM THE STORY "THE THUNDER RIDER" BY ROBERT E. HOWARD, CREATOR OF CONAN

AND NOW, HEEDLESS OF STYGIAN CURSE AND HYBORIA'S HATRED, THE PIRATE SHIP *TIGRESS* IS SAILING *NORTH* ONCE MORE-- TOWARD THE *CIVILIZED LANDS* THAT BIRTHED HER TWO DARK-MANED *MASTERS...*

...SO YOU HAVE MET *PUBLIO* THEN, MY BARBARIAN?

THAT SHIFTY-EYED *MERCHANT* WE GO TO MEET IN *MESSANTIA?* AYE...

...THOUGH I DIDN'T MUCH *LIKE* WHAT I SAW OF HIM BEFORE.

HE'S A *TREACHEROUS* DOG, BELIT!

I KNOW WE MUST *SELL* THE BOOTY WE'VE GATHERED, FOR *GOLD* TO FILL OUR COFFERS...

BUT WON'T SOME MORE *TRUSTWORTHY* MERCHANT GIVE YOU A *BETTER DEAL?*

NOT *LIKELY.*

HIS *FELLOW* TRADERS WOULD GIVE ME *NOTHING* AT ALL...

...AND, IN FACT, THEY WOULD TAKE *PUBLIO* SEVERELY TO TASK, IF THEY KNEW *HE* DEALT WITH ME.

WHY *NOT?* IT CAN'T BE SIMPLY A MATTER OF *COLOR.*

THE MERCHANTS OF ARGOS TRADE WITH THE *BARACHAN PIRATES*-- EVEN WITH THE RIVAL *ZINGARAN FREEBOOTERS*-- BUT NOT WITH MY *BLACK CORSAIRS!*

I'VE NEVER KNOWN A CIVILIZED MERCHANT WHO LET *RACE* STAND IN THE WAY OF A NICE FAT *PROFIT.*

NO, CONAN... IT'S *NOT* RACE, BUT *FEAR* THAT MOTIVATES THE MERCHANT FATHERS OF ARGOS--

FEAR OF A DAY A *HUNDRED YEARS GONE* NOW-- A DAY ALL BUT *FORGOTTEN* ON THE BLACK COAST WHEN *I* CAME THERE--

--THE DAY OF *AHMAAN!*

"*NO* HYBORIAN CITY WAS SAFE FROM HIS WILD-EYED *REAVERS...*

"...AND IT IS SAID THAT EVEN *BLOODY TRANICOS,* MOST RUTHLESS OF ALL THE BARACHAN PIRATES, AVOIDED HIS WHITE-CAPPED PATH! HE--"

"*AHMAAN THE MERCILESS,* THEY CALLED HIM.

"HE HAD BEEN A *SLAVE* IN ZINGARA, LEARNING ENOUGH THERE OF SEA-GOING TO LEAD HIS *OWN* BAND OF BLACK CORSAIRS WHEN HE *ESCAPED.*

GODDESS! SHIPS COMING UPON US-- FROM THE SHORE!

THREE SHIPS-- AND SWIFT ONES!

WHAT? LET ME--

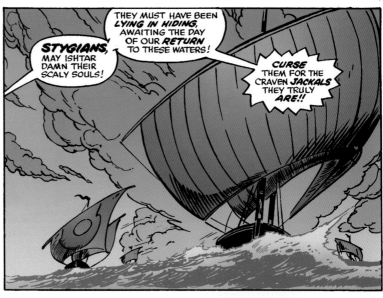

STYGIANS, MAY ISHTAR DAMN THEIR SCALY SOULS!

THEY MUST HAVE BEEN LYING IN HIDING, AWAITING THE DAY OF OUR RETURN TO THESE WATERS!

CURSE THEM FOR THE CRAVEN JACKALS THEY TRULY ARE!!

SAVE YOUR CURSES FOR A LATER DAY, WOMAN! RIGHT NOW, THERE ARE TOO MANY OF THEM FOR US TO FIGHT.

AYE! THEN, OUT TO SEA, MY CORSAIRS--

THE STYGIANS WILL NOT FOLLOW US FAR OUT OF SIGHT OF LAND!

GODDESS-- NO! NOT IN THESE HAUNTED WATERS!

LET US TURN AND FIGHT!

BETTER A CHANCE AGAINST THE STYGIANS-- THAN TO DEFY THE CURSE OF DAGON!

THE DEVIL WITH DAGON! WHAT DOES THAT LAND-HUGGING GOD MEAN TO SEA-WOLVES?

I AM BÊLIT--DAUGHTER OF THE DEATH-GODDESS DERKETA--AND MY ANGER IS HERE AND NOW, NOT WAITING BACK IN THE SILVER ISLES!

OUT TO SEA, I SAY--

--BEFORE THOSE SET-WORSHIPPERS ARE SWABBING THE DECKS WITH OUR BLOOD!

AND IF YOU NEED ANYTHING FURTHER TO PERSUADE YOU, LADS...

...THAT TOO CAN BE TAKEN CARE OF!

MOMENTS LATER...

AS *ONAHU* SAID, MY CONAN-- *THESE* WATERS IN PARTICULAR ARE *JUJU*-- *BAD MAGIC*--

--*HAUNTED*!

WE'LL SOON LEAVE THOSE DOGS *BEHIND*, BÊLIT, BUT, I DON'T *LIKE* THREATENING YOUR CORSAIRS. THEY'RE *BRAVE* MEN, MOSTLY...

WHY DO THEY FEAR THE *OPEN SEA*, MORE THAN *I*-- WHO HAD NEVER EVEN *SEEN* THE WESTERN OCEAN TILL RECENTLY?

FOR, IT WAS IN THESE VERY WATERS, THE STORIES SAY, THAT *AHMAAN THE MERCILESS* VANISHED, A CENTURY AGO...

...BRINGING THE *FIRST* AGE OF BLACK CORSAIRS TO A *SUDDEN END*!

WHAT *HAPPENED* TO HIM?

THE LEGENDS SAY HE SAILED TOO FAR, AND TOPPLED OVER THE *RIM OF THE WORLD*...

BUT, *N'YAGA* TELLS ME THE WORLD IS TRULY *ROUND*, AND *HAS* NO RIM-- AND HE IS AN *EDUCATED* MAN, SO--

MISTRESS--?

HO! SPEAK OF A *SHAMAN*, AND UP HE *POPS!*

WHAT BRINGS MY *MENTOR* FORWARD IN THESE ROCKY WATERS?

MISTRESS, I HAVE COME ON BEHALF OF THE *MEN*.

THEY WILL NOT *MUTINY* AGAINST YOU-- YOU *KNOW* THAT--

BUT, THEY ASK THAT YOU *TURN BACK*-- AND, FOR THEIR SAKES, I *TOO* THUS ASK IT OF YOU!

WHAT? I EXPECTED *BETTER* OF YOU, N'YAGA.

YOU'RE NOT JUST SOME SUPERSTITIOUS *SAVAGE*. YOU HAVE STUDIED IN THE *COURTS OF SHEM*. YOU HAVE *LEARNED*...

I HAVE *LEARNED*, MISTRESS, THAT WHERE THERE IS SUFFICIENT *SMOKE*...

BUT, BÊLIT STANDS *FIRM*-- WILLING TO RISK NO BATTLES WITH SCANT CHANCE OF *LOOT*--

...THERE IS OFTTIMES THE *DRAGON* THAT BREATHES OUT *FIRE!*

AND SO THE SHIP TRAVELS THRU THE *NIGHT*, WITH CLOUDS MASKING THE STARS SO THAT THEY CAN ONLY *GUESS* THE WAY THEY GO...

THEN, AS THE MISTS OF DAWN *RISE* AT LAST, A TOWERING *PEAK* CLEAVES THE SKY IN THE VERY PATH OF THE *TIGRESS*...

...AND THE BLACK CORSAIRS *STARE* AT EACH OTHER, AS IF THEY WERE *GHOSTS* IN THE MORN AFTER THE *DESTRUCTION OF THE WORLD*...!

WE MUST *NOT* GO ASHORE, GODDESS! IT IS A *JUJU PLACE*...!

SILENCE! WE NEED FOOD, SUPPLIES-- AND WE'LL *NOT* GET THOSE BY COWERING HERE ON THE *DECKS*.

I *MYSELF* SHALL LEAD THE EXPEDITION ASHORE, SO YOU' KNOW THERE IS NOTHING TO *FEAR*.

I'D THINK *TWICE* ON THAT, WOMAN.

I DON'T LIKE THE *LOOK* OF THE PLACE, SOMEHOW.

WHAT? IS *YOUR* SPINE TURNING TO JELLY, TOO? DON'T TELL ME THAT *YOU*--

WHOA, GIRL-- *SLOW DOWN!* I'LL WALK *BESIDE* YOU, AS ALWAYS-- YOU *KNOW* THAT.

BUT, TO FIND THE *ONE ISLAND* IN AN *EMPTY SEA*-- IT DOES SMACK OF *MAGIC*.

MAGIC CAN BE *GOOD*, AS WELL AS *BAD*.

NOW, LET'S *GO!*

ERE LONG, THE TIGRESS' *LONGBOAT* IS THRUST ASHORE, LIKE A *THORN* INTO THE ISLAND'S TENDER FLESH...

AND CONAN FINDS HIMSELF WONDERING WHETHER, AT LEAST AT *TIMES*, BÊLIT DOESN'T ACTUALLY *BELIEVE* THE TALES WHICH NAME HER A *GODDESS*...

...AND NOT SIMPLY A *SHEMITE GIRL* MADE TO LOOK DIVINE BY THE CRAFTY WITCH-DOCTOR N'YAGA.

IF SO, SHE'LL NOT BE THE *FIRST* PERSON WHO BELIEVED HER OWN LEGEND. NOR, HE SUSPECTS, THE *LAST*.

IT IS A *DIM, SULLEN* LAND, BÊLIT...

THE DUSKY *HAZE* OVER IT SEEMS LESS A *MIST*...THAN A LESSENING OF THE SUN'S LIGHT.

AS LONG AS THE *STYGIAN ARMY* ISN'T LURKING IN THOSE *TREES*...!

THERE ARE WORSE THINGS THAN *SWORDPOINTS*, WOMAN, AS YOU OF *ALL* PEOPLE OUGHT TO--

MOTHER OF *MITRA!*

ISHTAR'S *GIRDLE!*

A *STAIR-WAY*-- HEWN OUT OF LIVING STONE, AND LEADING RIGHT UP INTO THE *MOUNTAIN!*

THEN-- THIS ISLE *ISN'T* UNINHABITED, AS WE'D THOUGHT!

AND, BEING SO FAR OFF THE *SEA-LANES,* IF ITS PEOPLE HAVE ANY *TREASURE*-- IT'S DOUBTLESS NOT BEEN *PILFERED* YET!

SO MUCH THE BETTER FOR *US,* EH?

CROM TAKE ME, GIRL, I'VE NEVER SEEN *ANYONE* SO CONSUMED BY *GREED* FOR GOLD!

NOT *GREED,* CONAN-- BUT DESIRE FOR *REVENGE* UPON THE *SLAYERS* OF MY FATHER!

AND FOR *THAT,* I NEED *GOLD* TO--

GODDESS! AMRA!

NOW WHAT--?

AMRA! ALREADY, CONAN SENSES THAT THIS NAME-- WHICH HAS TAKEN HOLD EVEN AMONG THE BLACK CORSAIRS-- WILL BE THE ONE BY WHICH HE SHALL BE *EVER KNOWN* ALONG THE BLACK-COAST LANDS.

SHRUGGING HIS SHOULDERS IN SILENT ACCEPTANCE, HE STRIDES WITH BÊLIT TOWARD THE AWED VOICE...

LOOK YOU *BOTH!*

A *HUT*-- HIDDEN FROM *SEA VIEW!*

IT IS A *MEDICINE HUT*--A JUJU PLACE--

THERE IS *TRUTH* IN THEIR WORDS, BÊLIT.

SUCH A HUT WOULD *NOT* BE BUILT SO CLOSE TO THE SEA UNLESS FOR A *CEREMONIAL PURPOSE.*

BUT IT HAS THE LOOK OF *GREAT AGE* ABOUT IT.

AYE. AND, SINCE NO ONE SEEMS TO BE ANSWERING ALL THE *SHOUTING* WE'VE BEEN DOING...

...LET'S JUST SEE WHAT'S *INSIDE* THAT-- *CROM!*

WHAT *IS* IT, CONAN? LET *ME*--!

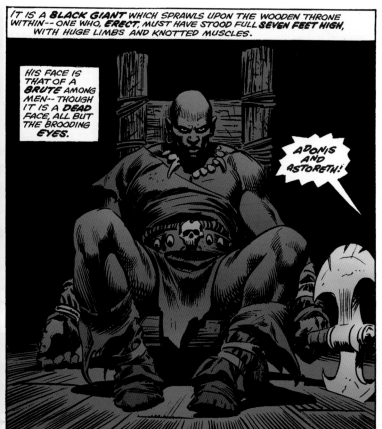

IT IS A **BLACK GIANT** WHICH SPRAWLS UPON THE WOODEN THRONE WITHIN-- ONE WHO, **ERECT,** MUST HAVE STOOD FULL **SEVEN FEET HIGH,** WITH HUGE LIMBS AND KNOTTED MUSCLES.

HIS FACE IS THAT OF A **BRUTE** AMONG MEN-- THOUGH IT IS A **DEAD** FACE, ALL BUT THE BROODING **EYES.**

ADONIS AND ASTORETH!

WHO IN THE NAME OF ALL THE DEVILS IN **SHEM--?**

DON'T YOU **KNOW,** MISTRESS? THIS CAN ONLY BE THE VANISHED **AHMAAN THE MERCILESS!**

AHMAAN-- THE LONG- DEAD--?

BUT, HE LOOKS AS IF HE DIED... ONLY **MOMENTS** AGO, NOT A **CENTURY!**

IT **MUST** BE HE! SEE THERE-- THAT GLEAMING **AXE** IN HIS HAND, SUCH AS THE **LEGENDS** TELL OF!

I MUST--

NO! IT IS I, **KAWAKU,** WHO SAW IT **FIRST--**

--AND IT MUST BE **I** WHO--

MANHOOD OF DAGON! I CAN NEITHER LOOSE THE DEAD GIANT'S **GRIP--**

--NOR EVEN **LIFT** THE AXE, FROM WHERE IT'S STUCK IN THE **FLOOR!**

BUT, IT DOES NOT BITE **DEEPLY** INTO THE WOOD THERE!

TRULY, THIS IS A **JUJU PLACE!** WE MUST **BEGONE** AT ONCE, BEFORE--

I ALREADY DEALT WITH YOUR PANIC ONCE **BEFORE,** KAWAKU. I'VE NO PATIENCE FOR DOING SO **AGAIN.**

NOW, **STAND ASIDE,** BOTH OF YOU--

--WHILE I SEE WHAT'S SO *SPECIAL* ABOUT THIS--

--AXE.

WHY, IT'S LIGHT AS A *FEATHER!*

SURELY, KAWAKU, YOUR STRENGTH IS BECOMING THAT OF AN *OLD WOMAN!*

NO, MY LOVER-- DON'T YOU *SEE*? KAWAKU COULD NOT LIFT IT BECAUSE HE IS *UNWORTHY.*

BUT IT YIELDED TO *YOU*, BECAUSE YOU ARE *AMRA*-- AMRA THE *LION*, MATE TO *BÉLIT!*

NO! IT IS *BAD JUJU*-- A *DEATH-HUT!*

SILENCE, YOU *FOOL!*

WOULD YOU INFECT THE *OTHERS* WITH YOUR *COWARDICE?*

THIS IS *NO* DEATH-HUT, WHERE WARRIORS LAID THE CORPSE OF A GREAT CHIEF. THIS MAN DIED IN HIS *SLEEP.*

WHY HE HAS LAIN HERE SO LONG WITHOUT BEING DEVOURED BY WOLVES OR BUZZARDS, I DO NOT *KNOW...*

BUT I *DO* KNOW I'LL HAVE THIS *AXE!*

NOW, WOMAN-- FROM THE BARE LOOKS OF THIS HUT, THERE'S NO *LOOT* HERE-- AND PROBABLY NONE OF THOSE *STONE STAIRS*, EITHER.

SO WE MIGHT AS WELL STOCK UP ON *FRESH WATER* AND SOME *FRUITS*, AND THEN HIGHTAIL IT BACK TO--

WHAT ARE YOU *STARING* AT?

OUTSIDE--!

CROM! IT SEEMS IF WE STEP *ONE* WAY, THINGS START HAPPENING EVERYPLACE *ELSE!*

LET'S SEE WHAT--

HOLY MITRA! I'LL RUN OUT OF *OATHS* BEFORE THIS ACCURSED DAY IS THRU--!

AYE, MY BARBARIAN-- AND PERHAPS OUT OF **SANITY**, AS WELL!

FOR, DOWN THE GREAT STONE STAIRWAY NOW POURS A **HORDE** OF SHORT BROWN FIGURES--WHIPLIKE ROPES OF **RAWHIDE** IN THEIR HANDS--

--A TALLER, **GAUNTER** MAN AMONG THEM, BEARING A SHIELD-SHAPED DISK OF **GLEAMING METAL** IN ONE HAND, A **COPPER MALLET** IN THE OTHER --!

NOISELESSLY, THE THRONG **APPROACHES**

HOLD! WE'VE COME IN **PEACE**-- AND WISH TO **DEPART** THE SAME WAY!

THE **DEVIL** WE DO!

WE'RE **OUT-NUMBERED** WOMAN! DON'T--

OUT-NUMBERED BY **PYGMIES**-- WHO WEAR BRIGHTLY-DYED **FEATHERS**!

THOSE **ALONE** WOULD GO FOR A PRETTY PENNY IN **ARGOS**-- AND THEY'VE DOUBTLESS **OTHER** TREASURES, AS WELL!

WE'LL MARCH THEM RIGHT BACK **UP** THOSE STAIRS, AND FIND OUT **WHAT--**

BUT, EVEN AS THE PIRATE QUEEN REACHES FOR HER **SWORD**, THE **GAUNT** MAN METHODICALLY SMITES **MALLET** AGAINST **GONG** --

--AND A TERRIBLE **CRASH OF SOUND** LEAPS OUTWARD, LIKE AN **INVISIBLE PANTHER!**

IT IS LIKE THE IMPACT OF A **THUNDERBOLT**--

--A THING NEARLY **TANGIBLE** IN ITS POWER--

AND, BEFORE IT, BÊLIT AND HER CORSAIRS **RECOIL**, AS IF STRUCK BY LIGHTNING--!

BUT, ONE MIGHTY-SINEWED FORM HAS BEEN STAGGERED *LESS* THAN THE OTHERS BY THAT TIDAL WAVE OF WONDROUS SOUND--

AND NOW, AS HE *CHARGES* AT HIS DUSKY FOEMAN, THE TALL ONE SEEMS TO ESPY HIS HUGE *AXE* FOR THE FIRST TIME...

AND, *ALSO* FOR THE FIRST TIME, HE REGISTERS AN EXPRESSION -- OF *SURPRISE.*

STILL, *ONCE MORE*, HE CLANGS THAT AWESOME GONG NO MORE FRANTICALLY THAN *BEFORE*...

...WHICH ONCE MORE HURLS BACK MAN AND WOMAN ALIKE, IN AN *AGONY* OF WRITHING MOTION!

THE SOUND *ENGULFS* CONAN NOW, SO THAT HE CANNOT HEAR HIS OWN DREAD *WAR-CRY* AS HE STRUGGLES PAINFULLY TO HIS FEET--

--AND *LEAPS*--

--TO GRASP THE *VULTURE-CRESTED MAN*--

--AND RAISE HIGH THE AXE WHICH NOW SEEMS BUT AN EXTENSION OF HIS OWN *HAND*

YET, THE GONG IS TAPPED ONE *FINAL* TIME...

...STILL EVER SO LIGHTLY...

...AND, HIS RESISTANCE UTTERLY *FLED* NOW, THE CIMMERIAN *FALLS* --LIKE A MAN BEATEN TO THE GROUND BY A *HEAVY CLUB!*

AT LENGTH, CONAN CAN *HEAR* AGAIN, AND *THINK*--AND *SEE*--

--AND *FEEL*--

--FEEL THE *RAWHIDE THONGS* WHICH BITE INTO HIS HANDS AND NECK--

BÉLIT--?

I AM HERE...

BUT, WE WON'T BE FOR *LONG*, NOW THAT *YOU* HAVE AWAKENED!

WHEREVER WE'RE BOUND, THEY EVIDENTLY WANT ME TO TAKE THIS *AXE* WITH ME--AS LONG AS I DON'T TRY TO CUT MY *BONDS* WITH IT!

WELL, *I* WON'T.. FOR *NOW*!

I SEE THEY WANT *YOU* ALONG, N'YAGA... AND DUMBSTRUCK *BAKTU*, AS WELL!

A *DUBIOUS* HONOR FOR US *ALL*, CONAN...

...EVEN THOUGH I DON'T KNOW IF *KAWAKU* AND THE OTHERS ARE *ALIVE*, OR *DEAD*!

UPWARD THE GRIM PROCESSION WINDS, TILL IT COMES TO A TALL GATEWAY CARVED WITH THE IMAGE OF A GREAT *FEATHERED SERPENT*.

CONAN *SHUDDERS* AT THE SIGHT... THOUGH HE COULD SCARCELY SAY *WHY*.

IS IT FROM THE *MEMORY* OF SOME HALF-RECALLED *TALE* WHICH HAS REACHED EVEN HIS OWN SAVAGE *NORTHLAND*?

HE DOES *NOT* KNOW.

SOON, IN A BROAD CIRCULAR ROOM, BEFORE AN *IVORY THRONE* HEAPED WITH FURS...

SO! AT LAST WE MEET THE *MASTER* OF THESE UNSPEAKING *DWARVES!*

WHO *ARE* YOU-- THAT YOU HAVE *DARED* TO SO DISHONOR *BÉLIT?*

HAH! YOU ARE LIKE A PAIR OF *WILD BEASTS*...

...AND THERE IS THE FIRE OF *KILLING* IN YOUR DARK EYES!

KNOW YOU THEN THAT YOU STAND IN THE PRESENCE OF *TEZCATLIPOCA*, LORD OF THE MIST!

BUT-- WHAT IS *THIS* I SEE BEFORE ME?

THE GREAT AXE OF *AHMAAN*, CHIEF OF THE BLACK-SKINNED PIRATES OF AN *EARLIER* DAY?

THEN-- YOU *KNOW* OF AHMAAN--?

KNOW HIM, WITCH-MAN? FAR *MORE* THAN THAT!

IT WAS I WHO *SLEW* HIM!

IT WAS *LONG* AGO, AS *YOU* RECKON TIME...

"...THAT THE DWARFISH INHABITANTS OF THIS ISLE SAW THE BLACK PIRATES COME ASHORE, LED BY THE GIANT CALLED *AHMAAN*.

"FLEEING AND HIDING, THEY FROM LANDS EVEN FARTHER TO THE *WEST*...

"...AND I *CAME*-- THOUGH THEY WERE LATER, PERHAPS, TO WISH I HAD *NOT*.

"I DID *PERSONAL COMBAT* WITH AHMAAN, WHOSE VAST BULK WOULD HAVE *OVERCOME* ANY NOT PROTECTED BY *GREAT MAGIC*.

"FOR A *DAY* AND A *DAY* WE FOUGHT...

"... MY *SORCERY* AGAINST HIS *BRUTE STRENGTH*...

"...TO BOTH *FALL* LAST TO THE GROUND, UTTERLY *SPENT*!

"YET, IT WAS I, *TEZCATLIPOCA* WHO RECOVERED *FIRST*...

"AND THAT SEALED THE *DOOM* OF AHMAAN AND HIS MEN!

AWAKING, I TOOK *COMMAND* OF THIS ISLAND, AND PLACED THE DEAD CORSAIR CHIEF AS AN *ETERNAL WARNING* TO INTERLOPERS!

BUT, I COULD NOT WREST HIS *AXE* FROM HIM-- OBVIOUSLY BECAUSE OF SOME *LONG-AGO SHAMAN'S SPELL* PLACED ON IT!

YET NOW, *YOU* HAVE BROUGHT IT TO ME, AND MOST *WELCOME*!

BUT-- ALL THAT HAPPENED A *CENTURY* AGO!

I AM *NOT* AS OTHER MEN, BARBARIAN!

AND *I* SAY YOU ARE!

SET ME *FREE*-- GRAPPLE WITH *ME*, BIRD-MAN-- AND WE'LL SEE IF EVER *AHMAAN* WAS MIGHTIER THAN *CONAN*. ALSO CALLED *AMRA*!

YOU *TEMPT* ME, LONGHAIR--AND I THINK YOU WOULD BE QUITE *SURPRISED,* SHOULD WE DO *BATTLE!*

YET, I HAVE NAUGHT TO *GAIN* BY IT, SO I *DENY* YOU!

IT IS THE *WOMAN* WHO *INTERESTS* ME...

FOR, WE'VE HAD *NO FEMALES* AMONG THIS *DYING RACE* FOR *MANY YEARS!*

SHE WILL MAKE A MOST *AMUSING SACRIFICE*--WHOSE PASSING WILL MAKE MAGIC TO PROLONG *ALL OUR LIVES!*

LET *GO* OF ME, YOU SWAGGERING *OSTRICH!*

DON'T *GIVE UP,* BÊLIT! I'LL *RETURN* FOR YOU--I SWEAR BY *CROM* I WILL!

BUT, THERE'S NO *ANSWER* TO HIS SNARLED VOW--NOT FROM THE *WOMAN*--

--NOR FROM THE *GRIMACING DWARVES*--

--WHO *TOSS* HIM *PELLMELL* INTO A *DARKENED CELL.*

THEIR MASTER'S *CURIOSITY* SATED NOW WITH REGARDS TO BRONZE-SKINNED INVADERS, HE'LL DIE *FORGOTTEN* IN THE DARK...

AND IS IT *HOURS,* OR EVEN *YEARS* LATER, THAT HE HEARS AN *AGONIZED* SCREAM--

--A SCREAM WHICH, MASKED BY COLD STONES, MIGHT BE *MALE* OR *FEMALE--* OR EVEN SOMETHING *NOT QUITE HUMAN?*

BÊLIT--!?

FOR ALL THIS TIME, CONAN HAS WORKED HIS BONDS, TILL HIS *WRISTS* ARE NEARLY RAWER THAN *THEY*...

AND NOW, IN ONE MIGHTY *SURGE* OF STRENGTH *UNDREAMED* OF BY THE *DWARVES*...

...OR EVEN BY THE *SLAYER OF AHMAAN*...

...HE IS *FREE!*

AAAHRR--!

89

YET, AN INSTANT LATER, HE IS FORCIBLY REMINDED THAT HE IS FREE ONLY OF HIS *PERSONAL SHACKLES*...

...AND THUS, NOT *TRULY* FREE AT ALL.

WHILE, *ABOVE*...

SO MEN STILL *DIE,* THE SAME AS *ALWAYS!*

YOU ARE *MAD*--SLAYING FOR NOTHING MORE THAN A *WHIM!*

MADNESS IS *ONE* WHIM I ALLOW TO *POSSESS* ME NOW AND THEN!

LONELINESS IS ANOTHER...!

UNTIE ME... AND YOU'LL BE LONELY *NO MORE!*

EVEN A MAN WHO HAS BECOME AS A *GOD* CAN KNOW WEAKNESS IN THE PRESENCE OF A BEAUTIFUL, UNTAMED *WOMAN;* YET, AT SUCH TIMES, IT IS BEST TO KEEP ALL *WEAPONS* LOCKED AWAY.

TEZCATLIPOCA HAS *FORGOTTEN,* AND LEFT HIS BLADE PROTRUDING FROM THE CORSAIR'S BODY, AND SO--

HERE, MAN-DEVIL--

I *SWORE* YOU'D BE LONELY NO MORE!

ARRGH--!

IT IS *STRANGE,* GIRL

SOMEHOW, I DID NOT THINK HE WOULD DIE SO *EASILY!*

STOP TALKING *NONSENSE,* N'YAGA!

NOW, IT IS TIME FOR YOU TO--

I WAS PLAYING *SHAMAN* AMONG SAVAGES, AND *SORCERER* IN SHEM, WHEN YOU WERE LESS THAN A *GLEAM* IN YOUR FATHER'S EYE.

I NEED NO *COMMANDS* TO GUIDE ME!

NOR DID I MEAN TO *GIVE* YOU ANY, OLD MAN!

THEN, WILD EYES BLAZING, THE SHE-PIRATE RACES THRU THE *CELLS* BELOW--

--IN SEARCH OF THE ONLY MAN SHE HAS EVER ALLOWED HERSELF TO *LOVE*--

--AND GIVES SILENT THANKS TO *ASTORETH* WHEN SHE *FINDS* HIM.

CONAN! WHY WERE YOU LOCKED AWAY DOWN *HERE*, INSTEAD OF SIMPLY *SLAIN?*

I DIDN'T FEEL LIKE *ASKING*, GIRL!

THANKS! NOW, LET'S--

THAT *SLITHERING* SOUND!

BEHIND YOU--!

THE *LIVING* FEATHERED SERPENT!

WITH ITS APPROACH, CONAN SUDDENLY *KNOWS* HIS INTENDED DESTINY...

FOR, EVEN SUCH A CREATURE AS *THIS* MUST SURELY *EAT!*

CONAN MAKES NO *OUTCRY* AS ITS COILS ENFOLD HIM...

HE SIMPLY STRETCHES OUT HIS *HAND*...

...AND THE KNIFE IS *THERE.*

YET, IT SEEMS A *PALTRY* THING, WITH WHICH TO STAB AWAY THRU LAYERS OF THICK *FEATHERS*--

--AND SLASH AFTER SLASH SEEMS TO HAVE *LITTLE* EFFECT.

YET, THERE ARE *FEWER* SHIELDING FEATHERS NEAR THE SNAKE'S GREAT *HEAD*--

--SO THAT, WHEN NEXT IT COMES *CLOSE*--

--A SINGLE HARD *SLICE* DOES WHAT MYRIAD JABS COULD *NOT!*

91

IT'S *DEAD!* NOW, WHAT OF THAT *TEZCATLIPOCA* DOG?

DEAD AS *WELL,* IN THE CHAMBER ABOVE!

THEN, LET ME RETRIEVE THE *AXE OF AHMAAN!*

MOMENTS LATER, IN THE DOORWAY OF THE THRONE ROOM...

CROM'S DEVILS! IF YOU *SLEW* HIM-- THEN WHO'S THAT BARRING OUR *WAY?*

ISHTAR!

ISHTAR IS MERELY AN *IDOL,* CAST IN WOMAN'S FORM!

I AM *REAL,* AND *ALIVE...*

...AND LESS EASILY *SLAIN* THAN MY SERPENT *FAMILIAR!*

I DON'T KNOW WHAT KIND OF A NICK *SHE* GAVE YOU, WIZARD--

--AS *USELESS* AS HER OWN!

BUT *THIS* ONE IS--

HOLY MITRA!

IT IS A PITY-- FOR *YOUR* SAKE, BARBARIAN--

--THAT YOU *DID* NOT *FLEE,* INSTEAD OF PLAYING THE *HERO!*

ARRGH--!

STAB *AWAY,* FOOL! A *HUNDRED* WOUNDS MEAN NO MORE TO ME THAN *ONE!*

AND ALWAYS, MY *FINGERS* TIGHTEN AROUND YOUR *THROAT...*

...FOR, THERE IS MUCH *PLEASURE* FOR ME IN WATCHING A *BRAVE MAN* PERISH!

NO! YOU'LL *NOT* KILL HIM--

--NOT WHILE *BÊLIT* LIVES!

YOUR RAKING *TALONS,* WOMAN OF THE WATERS--

--COULD SCARCELY BE MORE EFFECTIVE THAN THE *SEEKING BLADE!*

OMINOUSLY *SILENT* NOW, THE FEATHERED MAN TURNS BACK TO THE *TASK AT HAND...*

AND THE THRUSTING *STABS* OF CONAN'S KNIFE GROW *FARTHER BETWEEN* AND EVER WEAKER...

...TILL SUDDENLY, *BÊLIT'S VOICE* RINGS OUT ONCE MORE:

TEZCATLIPOCA! HE IS *COMING* FOR YOU!

AHMAAN THE MERCILESS IS MARCHING UPON YOUR STRONG-HOLD!

A *LIE!*

THE *DEAD* CANNOT *RISE!*

NONE THE LESS, HE *COMES!*

LOOK FOR *YOURSELF!!*

SOMETHING-- IN YOUR *VOICE--!*

BUT-- *NO!* IT CANNOT *BE!*

STILL, A POWER *GREATER* THAN HIMSELF PULLS THE LORD OF THE MIST...

...UNTIL HE GAZES WITH AMAZEMENT OUT THE *WINDOW...*

NO! IT IS A *LIE!*

A MAN MAY *LIVE NIGH FOREVER...*

...BUT THE *DEAD* CANNOT *RISE!*

YET-- *AHMAAN LIVES!*

I *COME* FOR YOU, *TEZCAT-LIPOCA!*

AHMAAN, LORD OF THE *BLACK CORSAIRS,* SEEKS A *DEAD MAN'S VENGEANCE!*

MESMERIZED BY THE STARTLING *SIGHT...*

...THE MIST-LORD *TOO-LATE* REMEMBERS...

...THAT HE *RELEASED* HIS HOLD ON THE BARBARIAN, WHILE STILL THE *BREATH OF LIFE* WAS IN HIM!

PERHAPS A *KNIFE* WON'T KILL YOU, DEVIL--

93

--BUT WHAT ABOUT THE ENCHANTED *AXE OF ANMAAN*??

CONAN'S ONLY ANSWER IS SPOKEN BY *SILENT RED MOUTHS*.

THEN--

CONAN! THE *CASTLE*--!

IT'S *CRUMBLING* ABOUT US--

--AS IF ONLY THAT *WIZARD'S WILL* WAS HOLDING IT *UP!*

RUN, GIRL, AS IF *DEVILS* WERE AFTER YOU--

FOR THEY SURELY *ARE!*

DOWN THEY RACE, TEZCATLIPOCA'S *DOOMED* STRONGHOLD TOPPLING *BEHIND* THEM--

--A SUDDEN RISING *MIST* HIDING IT IN ITS *DEATH-THROES!*

CONAN! *BÉLIT!* THANK THE *GODS!*

N'YAGA-- AND OUR *MEN*, AWAKE AGAIN!

BUT-- ANMAAN--!?

I GAVE HIM BUT A *SEMBLANCE* OF LIFE, AND ADDED MY OWN TRICKS OF *VOICE!*

WE NEED HIM NO MORE!

AS THE GIANT CORPSE *FALLS* FOR THE FINAL TIME, CONAN *SHUDDERS* INVOLUNTARILY...

...WONDERING IF PERHAPS THERE IS *MORE* TO N'YAGA THE SHAMAN THAN *MERE* FIERY *POWDERS* AND MURMURED *JUJU* TRICKERY.

BUT, TIME ENOUGH *LATER* FOR SUCH MUSINGS...

...WHEN THEY ARE ALL SAFE BACK ON BOARD THE WAITING *TIGRESS*, AND THE DYING ISLE OF MIST IS BUT A LOATHSOME *MEMORY*.

IT WILL ALL SEEM LESS REAL THEN, CONAN THINKS.

OR SO, AT LEAST, HE *HOPES*.

END

94

STILL, I RECEIVED *SOME* TRAINING IN ARCHERY AND HORSEMANSHIP WHEN I SOLDIERED AMONG THE *TURANIANS* A COUPLE OF YEARS BACK...

...AND NOT *ALL* THE THINGS THEY TAUGHT WERE LOST ON ME!

CLOSER TO CENTER-- BUT AN INCH *LOWER* WOULD HAVE PIERCED YOUR IMAGINED FOEMAN'S *HEART*.

I'M STILL GETTING USED TO THE *ROLLING OF THE SEA* BENEATH MY FEET.

ALWAYS AN *EXCUSE*, EH, MY LOVER?

IT'S *TRUE*, AS WELL YOU *KNOW*.

I'M *USED* TO THE WAYS OF THE SEA BY NOW...

BUT STILL, A FEW DAYS *ASHORE*, AND A BORN LANDLUBBER LIKE ME BEGINS TO *FORGET*...!

I SUPPOSE YOU'RE *RIGHT*, AT THAT.

AFTER ALL, YOU NEVER EVEN *SAW* THIS WESTERN SEA TILL A FEW *MONTHS* AGO--

--WHEN YOU FOUND IT A *BETTER* PLACE TO LIVE THAN AN *ARGOSSEAN DUNGEON!*

THERE! THAT'S HOW N'YAGA TAUGHT *ME* TO DO IT, IN THE *SILVER ISLES* FAR TO THE SOUTH.

BY ISHTAR, LET THAT RED-HAIRED WITCH *RED SONJA* TRY TO BEST *THAT* SHOT!

STILL *JEALOUS*, ARE YOU-- OF ONE WHO THINKS NO MORE OF ME THAN SHE DOES OF HER *HORSE?*

YOU WASTE YOUR ARROWS OF ANGER ON *PHANTOMS OF THE MIND*, WOMAN.

96

YOU'RE WRONG ON ONE *OTHER* POINT, AS WELL.

I *DID* BEHOLD THE WESTERN SEA ONCE *BEFORE* THAT FATEFUL DAY I JUMPED ABOARD A SHIP IN *MESSANTIA.*

YOU NEVER MENTIONED IT TO *ME!*

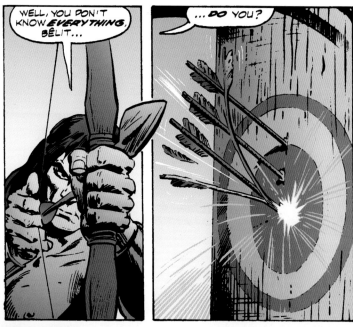

WELL, YOU DON'T KNOW *EVERYTHING,* BÊLIT...

...*DO* YOU?

ALL RIGHT, SO YOU'VE *IMPROVED* A BIT.

NOW, TELL ME ABOUT THIS EARLIER *SEA VOYAGE* OF YOURS.

IT WAS NO *VOYAGE*...BUT I DID *SEE* THE OCEAN.

IT IS NO *PRETTY TALE* WITH WHICH TO WHILE AWAY AN HOUR, THOUGH.

SINCE WHEN DID YOU EVER KNOW ME TO *WINCE* AT STORIES OF BLOOD AND SLAUGHTER?

THIS WAS *MORE* THAN THAT, WOMAN.. *MUCH* MORE.

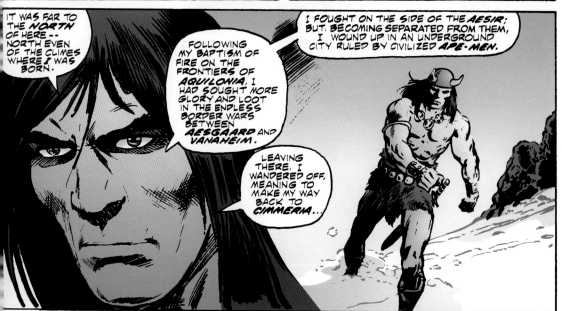

IT WAS FAR TO THE *NORTH* OF HERE -- NORTH EVEN OF THE CLIMES WHERE *I* WAS BORN.

FOLLOWING MY BAPTISM OF FIRE ON THE FRONTIERS OF *AQUILONIA,* I HAD SOUGHT MORE GLORY AND LOOT IN THE ENDLESS BORDER WARS BETWEEN *AESGAARD* AND *VANAHEIM.*

LEAVING THERE, I WANDERED OFF, MEANING TO MAKE MY WAY BACK TO *CIMMERIA...*

I FOUGHT ON THE SIDE OF THE *AESIR;* BUT, BECOMING SEPARATED FROM THEM, I WOUND UP IN AN UNDERGROUND CITY RULED BY CIVILIZED *APE-MEN.*

"MOST TIMES, I COULD HEAR A **SNOWFLAKE** DRIFT TO EARTH IN THAT WINTERY WASTELAND. BUT, THIS DAY, I MUST HAVE BEEN **CARELESS**...

"FOR, I FAILED TO SENSE THE **HUMAN EYES** STABBING INTO ME LIKE COLD **DAGGERS** FROM THE ICY **CRAGS** ABOVE...

"...TILL I WAS SURROUNDED BY A **VANIR WAR-PARTY!**

"THEY HAD NO MORE USED FOR **CIMMERIANS** WHO WANDERED INTO THEIR DOMAIN THAN THEY DID FOR **AESIR!**

"I SAW AT ONCE THEY WISHED TO **CAPTURE**, NOT **KILL** ME--AND THAT GAVE ME AN **ADVANTAGE**, SINCE I HAD NO SUCH QUALMS ABOUT SLAYING **THEM!**

"THEN, THE BLOW OF A **CLUB** STRUCK ME, EVEN THRU THE HELMET FORGED BY MY **BLACKSMITH FATHER**--

"--AND I RECALLED **NO MORE** FOR A TIME.

"**CROM**, BUT THERE WAS A **BATTLE** THAT DAY-- WITH NIGH A **DOZEN** OF THEM SEEKING TO OVERWHELM ME BY SHEER **NUMBERS!**

"THEN, *AWAKING*, I SCRAMBLED TO MY FEET-- TO FIND A *BLADE* AT MY GULLET.

"I DID NOT NEED TO ASK WHAT *FATE* AWAITED ME...

"FOR, I'D MET *OTHER* AESIR AND CIMMERIANS WHO HAD DWELT FOR *DECADES* AMONG THE GRUFF VANIRMEN...

"...AS *SLAVES!*

"PERHAPS I COULD HAVE *ESCAPED*; BUT I SUPPOSED THAT IN TIME THEY WOULD SEE THE VALUE OF MAKING ME A *COMRADE* RATHER THAN A *SLAVE*, SO I *PLAYED ALONG*, AND LEARNED WHAT I COULD...

YOU SAY, LIREIGH, THAT YOUR VILLAGE IS BY THE FABLED *WESTERN SEA*?

AYE. WHAT *OF* IT, BLACKMANE?

I JUST WONDERED *WHY*, THEN, YOU SPEND ALL YOUR TIME IN FRUITLESS *LAND-WARS* WITH THE *AESIR*.

AT *VENARIUM*, MONTHS AGO, I HEARD OF A BREED OF MEN TO THE SOUTH CALLED *PIRATES*, WHO--

WE *NEVER* GO TO SEA, SAVE TO *FISH*.

WHY *NOT?*

"HE WOULD NOT ANSWER.

"IN THE DAYS THAT FOLLOWED, AS WE TRAVELLED WESTWARD THRU THE VANAHEIM SUMMER, I TRIED *SEVERAL TIMES* TO SPEAK OF THE *SEA*, WHICH I HAD NEVER SEEN AND COULD NOT *PICTURE* IN MY MIND.

"BUT *LIREIGH*, THE VILLAGE'S WAR-CHIEF, REFUSED TO *SPEAK* OF IT-- OR OF WHY HIS PEOPLE HUGGED THE SHORE IN FRAIL *FISHING BOATS*, AS I'D HEARD FROM THE AESIR.

"THEN, ONE DAWN, ROUNDING A MOUNTAIN RIDGE, I SUDDENLY BEHELD--

THE WESTERN SEA!

"--AND *BY* IT, THE ROUGH *FISHING* VILLAGE OF LIREIGH AND HIS PEOPLE.

"BUT, FIRST *MY* EYES--THEN *LIREIGH'S*--FELL UPON A MILLING, STRANGELY SILENT *CROWD* AT WATER'S EDGE...

YMIR BLAST MY SOUL--!

HO THERE, THE *VILLAGE!* WHAT'S *WRONG??*

DAMN MY EYES, WHATEVER'S *GATHERED* THEM THERE, THEY'RE SO *SPELLBOUND* THEY DON'T EVEN *HEAR* ME!

SHOULDN'T A WAR-CHIEF *MAKE* HIMSELF HEARD?

AYE, *I'LL* MAKE MYSELF HEARD, ALL RIGHT--HEARD AND *FELT!*

STEP *ASIDE*, DOLTS, AND LET *LIREIGH* SEE WHAT--

YMIR'S FROSTY BEARD!

IT'S YOUNG *FALLON*--*DROWNED!* BUT *WHEN*--?

THIS *MORNING* ONLY, LIREIGH.

BUT HE MUST HAVE SUNK *DEEP*--FOR SUCH *WEEDS* DO NOT GROW EXCEPT FAR *BENEATH* THE WAVES!

STRANGE HOW HIS *CORPSE* DRIFTED ALONE BACK TO SHORE--AND SO *SWIFTLY!*

AND HE LOOKS SO *PEACEFUL*--MORE *ASLEEP* THAN DEAD.

MARGA, MY DAUGHTER--YOU WERE TO HAVE *WED* THE BOY.

TAKE HIM IN YOUR *ARMS*, LASS, AND *KISS* HIM--FOR THAT'S WHAT HE'D HAVE WANTED. *ALIVE!*

"THE GIRL *OBEYED,* DREAMLIKE. THEN, AS HER WARM *LIPS* TOUCHED HIS COLDER ONES, SHE SCREAMED AND *RECOILED--*

THIS IS *NOT* FALLON!!

WHY, WHAT DO YOU *MEAN,* GIRL?

THIS IS *NOT* THE BODY OF THE MAN I LOVED!

THIS IS SOMEONE-- *SOMETHING* ELSE!!!

HER *BRAIN* IS TURNED, POOR CHILD.

"I SAID *NOTHING,* FOR I WAS A STRANGER *AMONG* STRANGERS... AND A *CAPTIVE,* TO BOOT.

"BUT, YOUNG THOUGH I WAS, I COULD NOT IMAGINE A GIRL WHO WOULD *NOT* KNOW HER LOVER, EVEN IN *DEATH.*

"THEN, *LIFTING* THE SEAWEED-LADEN CORPSE, THE VANIRMEN BORE IT TO HIS *HOUSE--*

"-- THE HOUSE WHERE HE HAD HOPED TO BRING HIS *BRIDE,* ERE LONG.

"THE GIRL *MARGA* WALKED WITH THEM LIKE ONE IN A *TRANCE,* HER EYES STARING STRAIGHT AHEAD.

"AS THEY LAID HIS BODY DOWN, *SALT WATER* FROM HIS GARMENTS TRICKLED OFF THE BED AND SPLASHED ON THE FLOOR-- FOR, IT IS A *SUPERSTITION* AMONG THESE VANIR THAT MONSTROUSLY *BAD FORTUNE* WILL FOLLOW IF A DROWNED MAN'S *CLOTHES* ARE REMOVED.

"SHORTLY AFTER- WARD, EVEN AS I BEGAN TO *TIRE* OF THE DEATH- WATCH... SINCE I HAD NEVER *KNOWN* THE DEAD MAN...

SO! THEN IT'S *TRUE!*

AYE, GOWAR! YOUNG FALLON IS *DEAD.*

101

WHO'S *THAT*, LIREIGH?

I DON'T KNOW WHY I SHOULD *TELL* YOU, BEING AN OUTSIDER-- BUT THAT'S *GOWAR*.

HE'S A *REJECTED SUITOR* TO MARGA--AND A MOODY, *DANGEROUS* MAN WHEN CROSSED....!

SEA DEATH BRINGS A *CURIOUS CHANGE*, IF THAT'S THE *FALLON I* KNEW!

MACHA TAKE ME-- I DON'T THINK IT *IS*!

YOU *HATED* FALLON, GOWAR--AND YOU HATED MY *DAUGHTER* BECAUSE SHE PREFERRED A *BETTER MAN* THAN YOU!

NOW, BY *YMIR*, YOU'LL NOT BE *TORTURING* HER WITH SUCH TALK!

GET OUT-- AND *STAY* OUT!

I'LL *GO*, ALL RIGHT! OUT OF MY *WAY*, CAPTIVE DOG!

UNNN! SINCE YOU DON'T LIKE *CAPTIVES*, VANIRMAN--

--I'LL *BE* ONE NO LONGER!

NOW, WILL YOU LEAVE FATHER AND DAUGHTER *ALONE* IN THEIR GRIEF, OR--?

LET *GO* OF ME, YOU HILLBORN *OAF*, BEFORE I --

WHAT *WILL* YOU DO, GOWAR, PRINCE OF SNOW-JACKALS?

CROM'S DEVILS, BUT I'VE SPENT *LONG DAYS AND NIGHTS* WANTING TO SMASH IN A SMUG *VANIR* FACE--

--AND YOU MAY THANK ICE-BEARDED *YMIR* THAT YOU DON'T BECOME THE *SECOND* CORPSE IN THIS LODGE!

"YET, EVEN AS MY *FINAL BLOW* FELL, I KNEW I HAD *ERRED* IN SHOWING MY *TRUE STRENGTH.*

"DOUBTLESS I COULD HAVE *FLED* AT THAT MOMENT, AMID THE *CONFUSION* THAT REIGNED.

"BUT, SOMETHING *HELD* ME THERE..."

AND WHAT ABOUT *ME*, LIREIGH? I'VE FOUGHT ON THE *AESIR'S* SIDE AGAINST YOU.

WHY NOT LET ME FIGHT ON *YOUR* SIDE, IN THE FUTURE, *INSTEAD*?

I *LIKE* THE PROSPECT, LAD... SURELY I *DO!*

BUT, THE *COUNCIL* MUST PASS ON IT, NOT I ALONE.

"...SO THAT I MERELY *WATCHED* AS GOWAR'S FRIENDS HELPED HIM FORTH."

I *SWEAR* TO YOU ALL-- I MEANT WHAT I SAID *NOT* AS INSULT OR TAUNT!

THAT MAN IS *LIKE*-- YET STRANGELY *UNLIKE*-- FALLON!

MADNESS IS *CATCHING*, IT SEEMS.

AND *MEANWHILE*, I'LL FEEL BETTER WITH YOU *CHAINED*, THIS TIME..

103

"LATER, WHEN *NIGHT* HAD FALLEN, ONE BY ONE THE *LIGHTS* DIED WITHIN THE RUDE HUTS...

"...TILL AT LENGTH ONLY THE *DEATH-CANDLES* IN THE LODGE OF YOUNG, DEAD *FALLON* STILL GLIMMERED.

"AND AS FOR *ME?*

"*LIREIGH*, BLESS HIM, HAD HAD HIS WAY-- AND I WAS CHAINED TO A THICK *STAKE* JUST BEYOND THE TIDE'S REACH.

"*I* GAZED OUT OVER THE SLOWLY HEAVING EXPANSE, WHICH COILED AND BILLOWED LIKE SOME DROWSY *SERPENT*...

"AND IT SEEMED ALMOST TO ME AS IF THE SEA WERE A GREAT, GRAY, COLD-EYED *WOMAN*, SPEAKING TO ME IN THE SWISH OF THE FLAT *WAVES* ALONG THE SHORE-- IN THE WAIL OF THE *OCEAN-BIRD*, IN HER THROBBING *SILENCE*:

"*I AM VERY OLD AND VERY WISE,*' BROODED THE SEA; '*I HAVE NO PART* OF MAN.

"*I SLAY* MEN AND EVEN THEIR *BODIES* I FLING BACK UPON THE COWERING LAND...

"THERE IS *LIFE* IN MY *BOSOM*, BUT IT IS NOT *HUMAN LIFE*...

"MY CHILDREN *HATE* THE SONS OF MEN!'

" JUST THEN, A SUDDEN *SHRIEK* SHATTERED THE STILLNESS AND BROUGHT ME, CHAINED, TO MY *FEET*, GAZING WILDLY ABOUT ME --

AAAAAAA

"IT CAME FROM THE *DEATH-HUT*-- AND IT WAS A *GIRL'S SCREAM!*

"ALL THE VILLAGE CAME *RUNNING*--BUT I COULDN'T BREAK MY *CHAINS* AS I HAD THE *ROPES*...

LIREIGH!

WHAT DO *YOU* WANT, OUTLANDER? THAT *CRY*--!

--MIGHT MEAN *TROUBLE* YOU'LL NEED *MANY HANDS* TO DEAL WITH!

SET ME *FREE*, AND I VOW NOT TO *FLEE*--AT LEAST NOT *TONIGHT!*

I'VE HEARD CIMMERIANS SET *GREAT STORE* BY OATHS, SO--

THERE! NOW *COME ON!*

" *SECONDS LATER,* LIREIGH AND I HALTED WITH THE *REST* BEFORE THE SCENE OF *MURDER* AND *TERROR* THERE WITHIN THE *DEATH ROOM*...

MARGA--*DEAD!?* AND THE BODY OF FALLON-- *GONE??*

AYE, LIREIGH! WE *FOUND* HER HERE THUS--

--IN *GOWAR'S ARMS!*

WHAT *DEVIL'S WORK* IS THIS, GO *SPEAK UP*, MAN, OR I'LL--

IT WAS NOT *I* WHO KILLED HER-- EVEN THOUGH THEY *FOUND* ME HERE WHEN THEY CAME!

I *TOLD* YOU! SHE KNEW--AND *I* KNEW-- THAT IT WAS *NOT* FALLON, THAT COLD MONSTER FLUNG UP BY THE MOCKING WAVES!

IT'S SOME *DEMON* INHABITING HIS *CORPSE!*

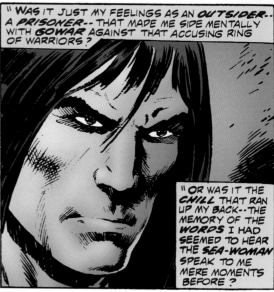

" WAS IT JUST MY FEELINGS AS AN *OUTSIDER*-- A *PRISONER*--THAT MADE ME SIDE MENTALLY WITH *GOWAR* AGAINST THAT ACCUSING RING OF WARRIORS?

" OR WAS IT THE *CHILL* THAT RAN UP MY *BACK*--THE MEMORY OF THE *WORDS* I HAD SEEMED TO HEAR THE *SEA-WOMAN* SPEAK TO ME MERE MOMENTS BEFORE?

UNABLE TO *SLEEP* AT THE THOUGHT OF MARGA SITTING BESIDE THAT COLD INHUMAN *THING* YOU THOUGHT HER LOVER, I ROSE AND CAME HERE.

EVEN AS I WATCHED IN HORROR, FALLON'S *EYES* OPENED-- AND THE CORPSE *SAT UP!* SHE HAD JUST TIME TO *SCREAM* ONCE --

THEN-- *BEARD OF YMIR* -- THE DEAD MAN *LAPPED* HER IN HIS TERRIBLE ARMS, AND SHE *DIED* WITHOUT ANOTHER SOUND!

AND WHERE *IS* THE CORPSE, GOWAR?

GONE, DAMN YOU! FLED INTO THE *NIGHT* JUST ERE YOU *CAME!*

YOU'RE A *LYING DOG!*

AYE! HE HAS *SLAIN* THE GIRL HIMSELF AND HIDDEN THE CORPSE SOMEWHERE TO *BEAR OUT* HIS GHASTLY TALE!

NO! I LOVED HER *TOO!* WHY WOULD I --?

HOLD!

MEN HAVE *DONE STRANGER* THINGS, IN THE NAME OF *LOVE.*

LIREIGH DO YOU *BELIEVE* THIS--?

IT IS A *STRANGE TALE* GOWAR HAS TOLD US-- AND DOUBTLESS A *LIE.* STILL, I'LL *NOT* HAVE HIM KILLED WITHOUT *CERTAINTY.*

HAVE YOU ANY *PROOF* OF WHAT YOU SAY, LAD?

LOOK AT HER, LIREIGH! DOES SHE LOOK LIKE SOMEONE THESE ARMS CRUSHED?

DOES SHE NOT LOOK, RATHER, LIKE SOMEONE WHO HAS--

--DROWNED?

DAMNED IF SHE DOESN'T!

I BELIEVE THIS MAN'S STORY, IF NO ONE ELSE DOES!

THUS, SINCE I'VE SWORN NOT TO FLEE THIS NIGHT, I'LL HELP YOU SEEK OUT THE GIRL'S TRUE KILLER!

YOU!? BY WHOSE RIGHT WERE YOU SET FREE??

BY MY RIGHT, STURLI -- AS WAR-CHIEF IN A TIME OF DANGER!

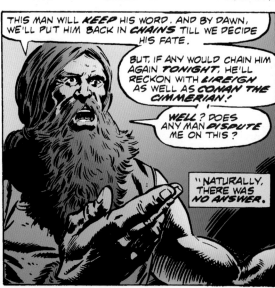

THIS MAN WILL KEEP HIS WORD. AND BY DAWN, WE'LL PUT HIM BACK IN CHAINS TILL WE DECIDE HIS FATE.

BUT, IF ANY WOULD CHAIN HIM AGAIN TONIGHT, HE'LL RECKON WITH LIREIGH AS WELL AS CONAN THE CIMMERIAN!

WELL? DOES ANY MAN DISPUTE ME ON THIS?

"NATURALLY, THERE WAS NO ANSWER."

"AND SO, LEAVING MEN TO GUARD THE SOBBING GOWAR, WE TURNED AWAY-- TO SEARCH AMONG THE SHADOWS FOR THE BODY OF YOUNG FALLON.

"I HAD NO SWORD... NOR, I SUSPECTED, WOULD IT HAVE DONE ME ANY GOOD TO HAVE ONE.

"THE MOON HAD GONE BEHIND A *CLOUD* AND I HAD BECOME SO *SEPARATED* FROM THE OTHERS THAT I COULD SEE NO LIVING SOUL"

"...WHEN SUDDENLY I HEARD A *SHOUT*..."

"...THAT BROKE INTO A *SHRIEK*..."

"...WHICH JUST AS SUDDENLY DIED OFF INTO A GRISLY *SILENCE!*"

" *LIREIGH* LAY *DEAD* ON THE EARTH--

"AND A *DIM FORM* SLUNK AWAY INTO THE GLOOM AS I CAME UPON HIS BODY, MY FLESH *CRAWLING!*"

LIREIGH! IS HE--?

DEAD.

IT'S *GOWAR* HAS DONE THIS DEED!

I JUST LEARNED HE HAS *ESCAPED* FROM THOSE WHO *WATCHED* HIM!

UNLESS IT IS *YOU*, BARBARIAN!

AYE, *THAT'S POSSIBLE!* AFTER ALL, HE *CAPTURED* YOU--!

I GAVE MY *WORD*--AND I *KEPT* IT!

" STILL, SEVERAL OF THEM STALKED *TOWARD* ME, THEIR SWORDS BEFORE THEM-- WHEN OUT OF THE *DARKNESS*--

AHEEEEE

ANOTHER DEATH- CRY!?

AND ONE YOU *CAN'T* BLAME ON *ME!*

GOWAR-- DEAD LIKE THE OTHERS!

AYE--JUST LIKE THE OTHERS!

HE TOO SEEMS A DROWNED MAN--AS DID LIREIGH!

" THEN, UNREASONING FEAR TOOK POSSESSION OF THE VANIRMEN, AND THEY FLED TO THEIR OWN HOMES--

" --TO LOCK AND BOLT DOOR AND WINDOWS AND CROUCH BEHIND THEM IN TERROR-- FOR WHAT WEAPON CAN SLAY THE DEAD?

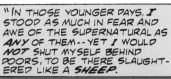

" IN THOSE YOUNGER DAYS, I STOOD AS MUCH IN FEAR AND AWE OF THE SUPERNATURAL AS ANY OF THEM--YET I WOULD NOT SHUT MYSELF BEHIND DOORS, TO BE THERE SLAUGHTERED LIKE A SHEEP.

" YET, IT WAS NOT COURAGE THAT SENT ME OUT INTO THE GHOSTLY NIGHT...

" ...BUT RATHER, THE DRIVING POWER OF A THOUGHT, WHICH HAD HAD BIRTH IN MY BRAIN AS I HAD LOOKED ON THE DEAD FACE OF LIREIGH.

" THUS, I STOLE THRU THE SHADOWS --TO PROWL ALONG THE BEACH ALL THRU THE DARK HOURS...

" AND, WHEN IN THE FIRST GRAY LIGHT OF THE EARLY DAWN, A FIENDISH SHAPE CAME STRIDING DOWN TO THE SHORE...

" ... I WAS WAITING FOR IT.

" TO ALL SEEMING, IT WAS FALLON'S CORPSE, ANIMATED BY SOME HORRID LIFE, WHICH CONFRONTED ME THERE IN THE GLOOM.

" THE EYES WERE OPEN NOW, AND THEY GLIMMERED WITH A COLD LIGHT, LIKE THE REFLECTION OF SOME DEEP-SEA HELL.

" AND I KNEW IT WAS NOT YOUNG FALLON WHO FACED ME !

SEA DEMON! I KNOW NOTHING OF YOUR DOMAIN--OR BY WHAT FOUL MAGIC YOU TWISTED YOUR DEVIL'S FEATURES INTO A LIKENESS OF THE VANIRMAN!

BUT THIS I KNOW.

SOON THE SUN WILL RISE, AND BEFORE THAT TIME YOU MUST BE FAR BELOW THE SURFACE !

THERE LIES THE SEA AND SAFETY; I ALONE BAR THE WAY!

"HE CAME *UPON* ME LIKE A TOWERING *WAVE*-- WITHOUT A *SOUND*, AND YET THE ROAR OF GREAT *BREAKERS* SEEMED TO ASSAULT MY INNER SENSES, FROM THE *LANDWARD* SIDE!

"HIS ARMS WERE LIKE GREAT *SERPENTS* AROUND ME. I KNEW THEY WERE *CRUSHING* ME--

"YET I FELT AS IF I WERE *DROWNING* INSTEAD!

"I TURNED *AWAY* FROM THE MONSTER'S INHUMAN *EYES*-- FOR IT WAS AS IF I GAZED INTO THE UNTOLD DEPTHS OF *OCEANS!*

"AND I FELT-- *SCALES!*

"NECK, ARM, AND SHOULDER HE *GRIPPED* ME, BENDING ME BACK TO BREAK MY *SPINE*--

"THEN, AS I *FOUGHT BACK*-- WITH A FURY WHICH, PERHAPS, ONLY ONE WHO HAS NEVER *KNOWN* THE SEA CAN WIELD AGAINST HER OR HER KIND-- THE CREATURE *ROARED* ONCE, THE ONLY SOUND I EVER HEARED HIM *MAKE*--

"AND IT WAS LIKE THE ROAR OF THE *TIDES* AMONG THE SHOALS!

"LIKE THE PRESSURE OF A HUNDRED FATHOMS OF *GREEN WATER* WAS THE GRASP UPON MY BODY AND LIMBS--

"AND THEN, AS I GAVE MY *FINAL EFFORT*, MY HEART NEAR *BURSTING* INSIDE ME, HE *GAVE WAY* SUDDENLY--

"--AND CRUMPLED TO THE *GROUND*, THERE IN THE SUN'S FIRST *GLEAMS!*

"HE LAY THERE *WRITHING* FOR A MOMENT, AND THEN WAS *STILL*...

"AND *ALREADY* HE HAD BEGUN TO *CHANGE*:

"*MERMAN*, THE ANCIENTS NAMED HIS KIND, KNOWING THEY COULD TAKE THE FULL FORM OF A *MAN*-- IF LIFTED FROM THE OCEAN BY THE *HANDS* OF MEN!

"IN MOMENTS, THE SUN'S FIRST RAYS FELL UPON A SLIMY AND MOULDERING MASS OF *SEAWEED*, FROM WHICH STARED TWO *HIDEOUS DEAD EYES*--

CROM!

"--A FORMLESS *BULK* THAT LAY AT *WATER'S EDGE*--

"--WHERE THE FIRST *HIGH WAVE* WOULD BEAR IT BACK TO WHENCE IT CAME: THE COLD JADE *OCEAN DEPTHS*.

"THE NIGHT WAS *OVER*, AND MY PROMISE TO *LIREIGH* WAS FULFILLED...

"BUT, I'D *NOT* SWORN NOT TO FLEE WHEN THE *MORNING* CAME, NOR DID I WISH TO *STAY* IN THAT ACCURSED PLACE, EVEN AS A *FREE* MAN.

I WAS CAPTURED BY THE *HYPERBOREANS* SOME WEEKS LATER-- BUT THAT'S *ANOTHER* STORY.

WHICH, IF IT'S AS AWESOME AS *THIS* ONE, IT'S A WONDER YOU'RE HERE TO *RELATE*!

BUT-- HOW DID YOU *KNOW* THAT THE MONSTER HAD TO RETURN TO THE *SEA* BY DAWN, OR ELSE BE DESTROYED BY THE *SUN'S FIRST RAYS*?

I *DIDN'T* KNOW. I *SENSED* IT, RATHER-- A SUDDEN *THOUGHT* THAT CAME TO ME OF *NOWHERE*.

PERHAPS THE *SEA*, STRANGE AND FICKLE EVEN TO HER *CHOSEN*, HAD WHISPERED SOMETHING TO MY *INNER MIND*-- BETRAYING HER OWN.

I *KNOW* NOT, NOR PERHAPS SHALL I *EVER*.

BUT, SHE'S STILL *OUT THERE*, THAT COLD GRAY *SEA-WOMAN* WHO CALLED TO ME IN THAT LONG-AGO NIGHT--

AND ONE DAY I'LL *SEE* HER FACE TO FACE--

--THOUGH *THAT'S* A TALE I MAY *NOT* LIVE TO TELL....

END

"Know, O prince, that between the years when the oceans drank Atlantis and the gleaming cities, and the rise of the sons of Aryas, there was an Age undreamed of, when shining kingdoms lay spread across the world like blue mantles beneath the stars.
"Hither came Conan, the Cimmerian, black-haired, sullen-eyed, sword in hand, a thief, a reaver, a slayer, with gigantic melancholies and gigantic mirth, to tread the jeweled thrones of the Earth under his sandaled feet."

—*The Nemedian Chronicles.*

Stan Lee PRESENTS: CONAN THE BARBARIAN™

THE CITY IN THE STORM!

A STORM AT SEA!

WHENEVER MEN START TO FEEL *FULL* OF THEMSELVES-- BEGIN TO BELIEVE IN THAT THEY ARE *MASTERS* OF THE SURGING OCEAN, INSTEAD OF MERELY *TRESPASSERS* ON HER WATERY DOMAIN--

--THE SEA TAKES HER *REVENGE!*

ALL RIGHT, YOU LUBBERS--LOOK *ALIVE* DOWN THERE!

BY ISHTAR, I'VE SEEN *WORTHIER* SAILORS RIDING *CAMELS* ON THE SAND-TRAIL TO *ZAMBOULA!*

ROY THOMAS, WRITER/EDITOR

JOHN BUSCEMA, ARTIST

and *JOHN COSTANZA,* letterer

FREELY ADAPTED FROM THE STORY "*MARCHERS OF VALHALLA*" by *ROBERT E. HOWARD,* CREATOR OF CONAN

CONAN! KEEP A TIGHT REIN ON THAT LINE, BLAST YOU--IF YOU DON'T WANT THE TASTE OF *BRINE* IN YOUR MOUTH!

WHAT'S ON YOUR *MIND* DOWN THERE? *RED SONJA*??

BY THE GODS, MUST I DO EVERYTHING *MYSELF*?

YOU CAN GRAB THIS *ROPE* ANYTIME YOU WANT TO, BÊLIT-- AND THAT'S FOR *SURE*!

M'GORA! KAWAKU! GIVE ME A *HAND* HERE!

WHAT'S *WRONG* WITH YOU, KAWAKU? DIDN'T YOU HEAR *AMRA*?

AYE, M'GORA! BUT--THE *SEA*-- IT ROARS IN MY *EARS*!

I HAVE NEVER *HEARD* IT ROAR SO-- AND I'M *AFRAID*!

IT IS TELLING US WE MUST *DIE*, FOR ROAMING SO FAR OUT OF SIGHT OF *LAND*! IT-- *UNNNH--*!

AND WHAT DOES MY *FIST* TELL YOU, *COWARD*?

HOLD ON, AMRA! I'M *COMING*!

AND LEAVING BEHIND AN *ENEMY*, M'GORA...

...ONE WHO NOW HATES *YOU*, PERHAPS, NEARLY AS MUCH AS HE HATES *CONAN*, WHOM THE BLACK CORSAIRS CALL *AMRA*!

SUCH HATRED SEEMS NO DOUBT A *SMALL* THING, WHILE THE *WINDS* HOWL LIKE HUNGRY WOLVES AROUND THE SEA-ROVING *TIGRESS*...

YET, STORMS AT SEA HAVE A WAY OF *SUBSIDING* MORE SWIFTLY THAN STORMS WHICH RAGE IN THE SOULS OF MEN.

BUT, *THIS* SEA-STORM, ALL THE SAME, LOOKS DESTINED TO *LAST* A WHILE--AND *MEN* TIRE MORE EASILY THAN RAMPAGING, MAST-HIGH *WAVES!*

CONAN!

NOW WHAT? DO YOU WANT TO WORK THE *TILLER,* TOO?

NO, MY LOVER-- *LOOK--!*

LAND HO!

CROM'S DEVILS! THE WAVES *HID* IT FROM OUR SIGHT!

AND WHERE THERE'S *LAND,* THERE'S BOUND TO BE--

-- *ROCKS!*

THEN, EVEN AS THE *TIGRESS* THREATENS TO *FOUNDER* WITH A GREAT HOLE IN HER SIDE, THE SEA-GODDESS SEEMS SUDDENLY *CONTENT* WITH THAT WHICH HER WRATH HAS WROUGHT...

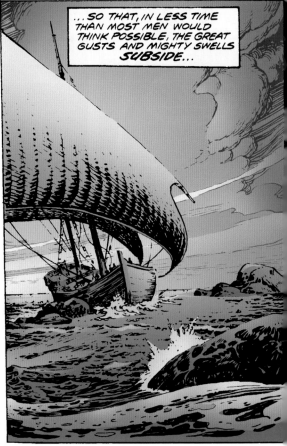

...SO THAT, IN LESS TIME THAN MOST MEN WOULD THINK POSSIBLE, THE GREAT GUSTS AND MIGHTY SWELLS *SUBSIDE...*

...LEAVING CAPTAIN, CONAN, AND CREW TO SURVEY THE *DAMAGE*:

HMMM...NOT AS BAD AS IT *COULD* HAVE BEEN! EASY TO FIX!

STILL, IF THE STORM HADN'T *ENDED* WHEN IT DID...!

I HATE TO KEEP *POINTING OUT* THINGS TO YOU, MY *BARBARIAN*...

...BUT, IT WOULD SEEM THE *ISLAND* WE'VE STRUCK IS NOT *UNINHABITED*!

CROM AND MITRA! THIS IS *MADNESS*!

A GREAT TOWERING *CITY*-- HERE, SO FAR OFF ANY TRAVELED *SEA-LANES*.!?

THE OCEAN IS *VAST*, CONAN. N'YAGA SAYS THE *SHEMITISH STAR-GAZERS* HAVE ESTIMATED THAT--

GODDESS! IT IS *ABOUT* N'YAGA THAT I HAVE COME. HE IS *HURT!*

ISHTAR! I MUST *GO* TO HIM!

I'LL GET WORK STARTED *HERE*, THEN JOIN YOU.

N'YAGA, YOU OLD FAKER! IF THIS IS YOUR WAY OF *SHIRKING--.*!

SPARE ME YOUR FRIENDLY *JIBES*, DAUGHTER OF SHEM.

I WAS *CARELESS.* A *TREASURE-LADEN CHEST* CAME LOOSE --LAID ME LOW.

BUT, I AM A MAN OF *SCIENCE* AS WELL AS A *WITCH DOCTOR*...

THUS, I HAVE PREDICTED THAT I SHALL *RECOVER*, GIVEN A FEW DAYS' *REST* AND A FEW *KIND WORDS.*

THEN YOU'LL HAVE *BOTH*, MY MENTOR.

AND I'LL SEARCH THE NEARBY *ISLE* FOR HEALING *HERBS* OF WHICH YOU'VE TOLD ME SINCE CHILDHOOD.

FROM THE DECKS OF THE *TIGRESS*, IT SEEMED PERHAPS THAT THE SIGHT THEY SAW WAS A *GHOST CITY*--

--A *MIRAGE*, WHICH WOULD *VANISH* WITH THE FIRST OAR TO STRIKE ALIEN SOIL.

YET, AMID THE LONGBOATS NOW, THERE IS *NO TALK* OF MIRAGES...

AND, WHEN WHITE AND BLACK PIRATES STEP *ASHORE*, ALL DOUBTS ARE LAID TO REST...

THIS IS *NO* GHOST CITY, CONAN, BORN OF SUN AND SILENCE.

NO. IT LOOKS INCREDIBLY *ANCIENT*, SOMEHOW...

...THOUGH BARELY *SCARRED* BY WIND AND TIME. IT--

AT THAT MOMENT, THE *MIGHTY GATES* SWING OPEN, AND OUT FILE LINES OF APISH *WARRIORS*, WITHOUT A SOUND.

MANHOOD OF ADONIS! THEY ARE *SAVAGES*-- BRUTES ARMED ONLY WITH *SPEARS*, AND LOOKING AS MUCH LIKE *BEASTS* AS MEN!

SURELY SUCH AS *THEY* NEVER BUILT THOSE GLEAMING TOWERS!

THAT HARDLY MATTERS RIGHT *NOW*, GIRL.

LOOK. THEY'RE *HALTING*...

SMALL *WONDER!* THERE ARE SCARCELY AS MANY OF *THEM* AS THERE ARE OF *US.*

AT LEAST THEY SEEM TO HAVE NO *MAGIC,* LIKE THOSE DEVILS ON THE *LAST* ISLE WHERE WE BEACHED!

WE'RE *VULNER-ABLE,* THE TIGRESS HAVING A *HOLE* IN HER SIDE.

SO, PERHAPS IT WILL BE *GOOD* IF WE MAKE *FRIENDS* WITH THEM, INSTEAD OF--

ISHTAR!

THE ONE TIME IN YOUR LIFE YOU TRY TO BE *PEACEABLE,* WOMAN--

--AND IT TURNS OUT TO BE THE *WRONG* TIME!

THE WRONG TIME NOT ONLY FOR *ME,* MY BARBARIAN--

--BUT FOR *THEM,* AS WELL!

AT LAST, THE CORSAIRS LEARN THAT THE ISLE'S INHABITANTS CAN SPEAK, AFTER ALL...

117

AND, SECONDS LATER, THERE ARE *VOICES A-PLENTY* ON THE SHORE BEFORE THE ANTIQUE CITY:

CRIES OF SAVAGERY AND *SLAUGHTER--*

SNARLS OF SHEER, UN-ADORNED, AND SIMPLE *HATRED--*

--AYE, AND HOWLS OF SOUL-WRENCHING *PAIN,* AS HARDENED PIRATES MEET UNDISCIPLINED WARRIORS!

BUT, THE BATTLE IS *SHORT--* AND THEN THE DEFENDERS *RUSH BACK* AT A GIVEN SIGNAL INTO THEIR CITY --

--SHUTTING THEIR GREAT GATES BEHIND THEM.

BY *BEL,* GOD OF ALL THIEVES! I DIDN'T THINK IT WOULD BE SO *EASY.*

MAYBE THEY STILL HAVE A *PLAN,* BÊLIT.

MAYBE --

YES, I SUDDENLY SUSPECT THEY *DO* HAVE A PLAN OF SORTS.

AND I DON'T *LIKE* IT--NOT ONE *BIT!*

BUT THEN, I'M DOUBTLESS *PREJUDICED* AGAINST PLANS THAT HAVE *GOLDEN HAIR* BLOWING FREE IN THE WIND --AND *MILKY WHITE SKIN* GLEAMING IN THE SUNLIGHT!

HOLD, STRANGERS! MY *MASTERS* HAVE A *WORD* FOR YOU!

SHE SPEAKS THE BLACK COAST TONGUE *STUMBLINGLY* -- AS IF SHE HAS NOT *USED* IT IN MANY A YEAR...!

WELL, BY *DAGON*, SHE'LL NOT USE IT *AGAIN*-- EVER!

KAWAKU--!

YOU'RE TOO *BRAVE* FROM A *DISTANCE*--

--AND TOO *CRAVEN* UP *CLOSE*!

OWWWWW

AGREED. WE SHOULD *LISTEN* TO THIS WOMAN...

...THIS WOMAN SO OBVIOUSLY FROM THE *NORTH*, WHO DWELLS AMONG *APISH SAVAGES*.

BUT HEAVEN *HELP* HER AT THE FIRST *SPEAR* LOOSED FROM ATOP THOSE WALLS!

DON'T TRY TO GRAB *MY* WRIST, CONAN!

THERE WILL BE *NO* SPEAR. THIS IS THE CITY OF *KELKA*.

MY MASTERS SAY: IF YOU SEEK TO *TAKE* THE CITY, THEY WILL FIGHT YOU TO THE *DEATH*.

BUT, IF YOU WILL *SPARE* IT, THEY WILL SEND YOU OUT *GIFTS* SUCH AS YOU HAVE SELDOM BEHELD.

LET'S SEE THE *GIFTS*!

AND, MOMENTS LATER, THEY *DO* -- AS A *PROCESSION* FILES OUT, LADEN WITH GOLDEN VESSELS CONTAINING FOOD AND WINES, GOLD AND JEWELS IN RESPLENDENT ARRAY...

...WHILE THOSE WHO *CARRY* THESE THINGS ARE NIGH CRAFTED TO TAKE THE MALE EYE *OFF* THE GIFTS THEY BRING.

FINALLY, FLANKED BY GRIMLY SILENT WARRIORS --

HAIL, WAYFARERS! I AM *AKKHEBA*, PRIEST OF *ASHTORETH*, GODDESS OF KELKA.

LET US BE *FRIENDS!* FOR WE'VE *GOLD*, WHICH WE SCARCELY *NEED* ON THIS ISOLATED ISLAND...

...AND YOU'VE *SWORDS* AND STRONG *ARMS*, WHICH WE *DO* NEED, THERE BEING *FEW* OF US.

ASHTORETH? SHE'S A GODESS OF MY NATIVE *SHEM!*

BUT OF *KELKA*, FIRST AND *FOREMOST*, DEAR LADY.

BARGAINING WITH US ALREADY?

LET HIM *TALK!*

WE KNOW DIMLY OF THE *BLACK CORSAIRS* OF OLD. BUT, *OUR* FOES ARE THE FIERCE *BARACHAN PIRATES*, FROM THE ISLES OFF *ARGOS!*

--TO EXACT A *TRIBUTE* FROM US, WHICH EACH YEAR GROWS *GREATER*.

AND YOU WANT *US* TO FIGHT YOUR *BATTLES* FOR YOU?

WELL, I'VE BEEN A MERCENARY *BEFORE*, AND MAY BE *AGAIN*.

I SAY, WE MAY AS WELL EARN SOME *GOLD* WHILE WE'RE HERE.

BUT, TO AVOID OBVIOUS *TEMPTATIONS*, NO MAN FROM THE *TIGRESS* WILL *ENTER* THE CITY.

NO MAN.

EACH YEAR AT THIS TIME, THEY COME HERE IN *FORCE* --

WHAT SAY *YOU*, BÊLIT? IT'S *YOUR* SHIP.

AND, BÊLIT *ENFORCES* HER DICTUM, BY KEEPING THE CORNER OF AN EYE ON HER BARBARIAN PARA-MOUR BY *DAY*...

...AS WELL AS BY *NIGHT*, OF COURSE.

THE MEN *WORK HARD*-- BUT THEY'RE *RESTLESS*.

SOME WHISPER OF SNEAKING INTO THE *CITY* TO HAVE SOME *FUN*.

AND THEY'LL *HOWL*, IF I CATCH THEM *NEAR* IT.

IT *SEEMS* THOUGH, THAT *YOU'LL* NOT HAVE THAT PROBLEM; HERE COMES THAT *BLONDE-HAIRED SHE-CAT*.

NOR IS IT LIKELY SHE'S HERE TO SEE *ME*.

I THINK I'LL TAKE A *STROLL* ALONG THE *BEACH*.

I WISHED YOU TO HAVE THIS *CARVEN KNIFE*, MAN FROM THE SEA... A GIFT FROM ME ...FROM *ALUNA*, HANDMAIDEN OF *ASHTORETH*.

MY *THANKS*, ALUNA, AND MY NAME IS *CONAN*--

--THOUGH THE *BLACK COAST* PER-SISTS IN CALLING ME *AMRA*.

COME. I'LL SHOW YOU WHAT A *PIRATE SHIP* LOOKS LIKE, UP CLOSE.

NO, I... *CANNOT*. MY MISTRESS *ASH-TORETH*--

SHE'S A *GODDESS*-- AN IMAGE IN A *TEMPLE*.

NO, SHE IS... *MORE* THAN THAT.

SHE DWELLS IN THAT *TOWER*-- THOUGH NOT EVEN *I* HAVE EVER *SEEN* HER FACE TO FACE!

THEN *HOW* THE DEVIL DO YOU KNOW SHE--?

WHILE YOU TWO PALAVER, MY *SHIP* IS LEAKING!

I MUST *GO*, IN ANY EVENT.

THAT WAS *UNCALLED FOR*, GIRL. SINCE WHEN HAVE I SOUGHT OUT ANOTHER WOMAN SINCE I TOOK UP WITH *YOU*?

SINCE WHEN DID I GIVE YOU A *CHANCE*? I--

121

GODDESS! IT COMES!

A SHIP COMES!!

THE NEXT MOMENT, IT IS APPARENT THAT THE PRIMITIVE-APPEARING MEN OF *KELKA*, TOO, HAVE SEEN THE SAIL -- AS A STRANGE, LOUD, YET MOURNFUL *TRUMPET* SOUNDS THE ALARM, HIGH ATOP THE CITY WALL...

IT'S A *BARACHAN SHIP* ALL RIGHT! NONE BUT A *PIRATE SHIP* FROM THOSE HATED ISLANDS WOULD SHOW THE *BLACK FLAG!*

M'GORA-- HAND ME THE *MAGIC GLASS!*

WHAT'S THERE TO *SEE*, GIRL? A PIRATE'S A *PIRATE*.

NOT WHEN YOU'VE SAILED THE COASTS AS LONG AS *I* HAVE, MY LOVER.

AYE, IT'S JUST AS I *SUSPECTED!*

THAT *GOLDEN BEARD*-- RARE AMONG MEN FROM *ARGOS*, SUCH AS MOST BARACHAN DOGS ARE--

IT CAN ONLY BELONG TO *AURO*-- THE MOST *FEARED* OF THAT LOOSE-KNIT BAND!

THEY SAY THERE'S NOT A *ZINGARAN BUCCANEER* VESSEL THAT DOESN'T *TURN TAIL* AT SIGHT OF HIS SHIP!

WELL, *WE'LL* TURN -- BUT NOT FOR *LONG*.

ALL RIGHT, YOU CORSAIRS --INTO THE *CITY*, FOR THE MOMENT!

WE'LL GIVE THAT YELLOW-HAIRED MONGREL A *WARMER* RECEPTION THAN HE'S GOT AT KELKA FOR *MANY* A YEAR!

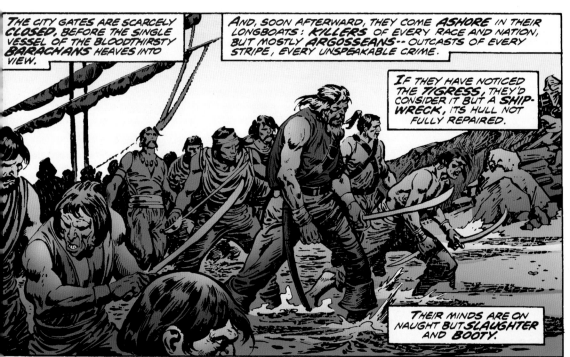

THE CITY GATES ARE SCARCELY CLOSED, BEFORE THE SINGLE VESSEL OF THE BLOODTHIRSTY BARACHANS HEAVES INTO VIEW.

AND, SOON AFTERWARD, THEY COME ASHORE IN THEIR LONGBOATS: KILLERS OF EVERY RACE AND NATION, BUT MOSTLY ARGOSSEANS-- OUTCASTS OF EVERY STRIPE, EVERY UNSPEAKABLE CRIME.

IF THEY HAVE NOTICED THE TIGRESS, THEY'D CONSIDER IT BUT A SHIP-WRECK, ITS HULL NOT FULLY REPAIRED.

THEIR MINDS ARE ON NAUGHT BUT SLAUGHTER AND BOOTY.

THUS, ON THE PLAIN, THE GREAT BLOND GIANT CALLED AURO SPEAKS:

NO, MEN OF KELKA! THE TIME IS COME 'ROUND ONCE MORE!

SEND DOWN THE TREASURE YOUR GEMSMITHS HAVE WROUGHT THIS YEAR, AS USUAL, AND WE'LL GO OUR--

THIS IS THE ONLY PLUNDER YOU'LL GET FROM US!

AN ARROW! BUT--THE KELKANS USE ONLY SPEARS.

AND, THAT VOICE-- IT HAS A NORTHERN CAST! WHO THE DEVIL--?

THE DYING PIRATE DOES NOT CARE WHOSE VOICE IT WAS ...

NOR, SOON, WILL THE BARACHANS, AS THE MORNING SUN SHINES DOWN ON DOZENS OF WELL-SINEWED EBON FORMS--

--AND, AMID THEM, TWO LIGHTER FIGURES, WHOSE FIERCE WAR-SHOUTS ARE FULLY AS SAVAGE AS ANY THAT EVER SPLIT A DARK JUNGLE NIGHT!

THE BARACHAN RENEGADES *OUTNUMBER* THE CORSAIRS FROM THE SOUTHERN ISLES...

YET, SUCH IS THE NEWCOMERS' STUNNED *SURPRISE* AT THE SIGHT OF THEM, THAT A RIPPLE ALMOST RESEMBLING *FEAR* SEEMS TO RUN THRU THEM LIKE A *SHOCK WAVE.*

AND, NO LESS *UNNERVING* A SIGHT IS THE HELL-CARVED IMAGE OF A BRONZED, UNTAMED *BARBARIAN* IN THE FORE-FRONT OF THE BATTLE--

--HIS DARK *CHAIN MAIL* MAKING HIM ALL BUT *IMPERVIOUS* TO THE PIRATES' ATTACK, SO THAT HE CAN RALLY THE *CORSAIRS* ABOUT HIM WITH FLAVOR-SPICED WORDS OF *ENCOURAGEMENT.*

DISDAINFUL OF ARMOR, YET NO LESS FEARSOME, IS *BÊLIT,* SELF-CROWNED QUEEN OF THE BLACK COAST...

...WHO HAS FOUGHT BOTH BARACHAN AND ZINGARAN *ALIKE* BEFORE, AND LIVED TO TELL THE TALE...

...EVEN WHILE SHE WIPED THE *BLOOD* OFF HER SWORD!

124

AURO IS A *BRAVE* MAN; STILL, ONE SELDOM GETS TO BE A *CAPTAIN* AMONG THE HIGHLY-COMPETITIVE BARACHANS IF ONE IS AN UTTER *FOOL.*

THUS, WHEN HE SEES THAT HIS *OWN* LOSSES FAR EXCEED THOSE OF HIS *ATTACKERS...*

IT'S *BÊLIT--* AND HER *MATE* THE ONE THEY CALL *AMRA!*

THE BOOTY HERE'S TOO *EXPENSIVE* FOR MY *TASTE,* LADS.

BACK TO THE *PETREL,* AND *HURRY!*

THERE ARE LESS *PROTECTED* CITIES TO LOOT!

THEY'RE *FLEEING,* CONAN! WE'VE *WON!*

SO IT WOULD *SEEM.* STILL, DON'T TURN YOUR *BACK* ON THEM WHILE THEY'RE STILL *SWORD-THROWING* RANGE.

THERE'S NO MORE *HONOR* IN THEM THAN IN A PACK OF THIEVING *JACKALS.*

BUT, A FINAL FURTIVE *THRUST* OR TWO IS THE *LAST* THING ON THE BARACHANS' MINDS, AS STRONG BACKS MAKE GOOD TIME BACK TO THEIR *OWN* SHIP...

...AND THE *PETREL* SETS SAIL WITH NO MORE THAN A *BACKWARD GLANCE...*

...AND A FEW MUTTERED *OATHS,* WHICH MAY OR MAY *NOT* BE WORTH RECOUNTING.

THAT OUGHT TO CONVINCE EVEN *YOU,* MY BAR-BARIAN.

IT *DOES,* FOR THE MOMENT. STILL, WE'VE PAID A *PRICE* FOR THIS *HIRED VICTORY.*

GOOD MEN ARE *SCARCE,* THIS FAR NORTH OF YOUR SILVER ISLES.

AYE! WHERE'S M'GORA?

I'LL HAVE HIM TAKE A DETAIL OF *MEN*, AND BUILD *PYRES* TO--

DO NOT *WEARY* YOURSELVES FURTHER, GREAT DEFENDERS OF OUR CITY!

AKKHEBA!

LET OUR MEN *HELP* WITH YOUR DEAD-- AND OUR WOMEN APPLY SOOTHING *BALMS* TO YOUR *WOUNDED.*

I'LL LIFT A FLAGON TO *THAT!*

STILL, WE CAN ATTEND TO THESE THINGS *BETTER,* IF YOU'D BUT ACCOMPANY US *INTO* THE CITY.

THEN, WE'LL *COME* WITH YOU; SOME OF THESE MEN NEED *ATTENTION.*

THAT THEY *DO!* BUT I GAVE ORDERS...!

AND I'M COUNTER-MANDING THEM!

BLAST YOU, WOMAN--NO GREEN-EYED *GARGOYLE* IS GOING TO CAUSE THE DEATH OF EVEN *ONE* OF YOUR LOYAL CORSAIRS, WHILE *I'M* YOUR SECOND-IN-COMMAND.

YOU'RE *RIGHT--* AND I'M *ASHAMED.*

ALL RIGHT, I *WITH-DRAW* MY EARLIER ORDER.

GLAD TO *HEAR* IT.

BEHOLD, YOU WHOM YOUR CORSAIRS CALL A *GODDESS,* AND YOUR MATE A *LION...*

BEHOLD THE *SPLENDOR OF KELKA,* A CITY WHICH HAS HAD *LITTLE TRAFFIC* WITH THE OUTSIDE WORLD FOR LONG YEARS...

...BUT WHICH CONTAINS MUCH TO *INTEREST* THOSE WHO'VE BEEN LONG WEEKS OUT AT *SEA,* EH?

INDEED IT *DOES* -- AND SOON, THE APISH *MEN OF KECKA* ARE MINGLING FREELY WITH THE *BLACK CORSAIRS*, WHILE THE CITY'S BEAUTEOUS WOMEN *DANCE* IN WILD ABANDON...

AND THE *WINE* FLOWS EVEN MORE FREELY THAN THE *FELLOWSHIP*.

POUR ME SOME *MORE* OF THAT PANTHER SWEAT, GIRL.

CROM TAKE ME, I'M STARTING TO *LIKE* IT.

EVERYONE IN THE *CITY* IS HERE, IT SEEMS.

WHICH *REMINDS* ME -- AKKHEBA, WHERE'S *ALUNA*, THE TEMPLE MAID YOU SENT TO US BEFORE WE GOT USED TO EACH OTHER'S *ACCENTS?*

CONAN -- SO *HELP* ME --!

I'M JUST *CURIOUS*, THAT'S ALL.

ALUNA IS AT PRESENT *OCCUPIED* WITH HER *DUTIES*, AND THUS COULD NOT JOIN IN OUR REVELS...

BUT, REST ASSURED, YOU'LL *SEE* HER ON THE MORROW, WHEN YOU VISIT OUR *TEMPLE*.

NO THANKS! I STAY AS FAR AWAY FROM TEMPLES AS I --

SLEEPY ALREADY, GIRL? YOU NEVER *COULD* HOLD YOUR LIQUOR.

THAT'S... SO MUCH *BULLROAR!* WE'VE HAD... A *HARD* DAY, THAT'S ALL.

SLAUGHTER... IS DIFFICULT... WORK...!

THE NEXT MOMENT, SHE IS ASLEEP...

AND, AS HE GLANCES OVER HIS COMRADES OF THE SEA, HE SUDDENLY NOTICES--

MITRA! THEY'RE DROPPING OFF LIKE FLIES!

BÊLIT--BÊLIT! WAKE UP, DAMN YOUR HIDE!

THERE'S... SOMETHING FOUL HERE! I--

NO USE!

FOOLS THAT WE WERE-- WE'VE BEEN BETRAYED!

THE WINE--IT WAS DRUGGED!

CAN'T EVEN STAND UP-- ANY MORE--?

MY SWORD! IF I CAN--

BUT YOU CANNOT, DOG!

OR ELSE MY SUBJECTS WOULD BE FORCED TO RUN YOU THRU WITH THE SPEARS THEY HAD SECRETED ABOUT THE HALL--

--WHEN, IN TRUTH, WE HAVE PLANS FOR YOU AND YOUR WOMAN--AYE, AND FOR THE BLACK CORSAIRS--

--WHEN ALONGSIDE THE GIRL ALUNA--

--YOU ARE SACRIFICED TO THE GREAT GODDESS ASHTORETH!

TO BE CONTINUED...

128

"Know, O prince, that between the years when the oceans drank Atlantis and the gleaming cities, and the rise of the sons of Aryas, there was an Age undreamed of, when shining kingdoms lay spread across the world like blue mantles beneath the stars.

"Hither came Conan, the Cimmerian; black-haired, sullen-eyed, sword in hand, a thief, a reaver, a slayer, with gigantic melancholies and gigantic mirth, to tread the jeweled thrones of the Earth under his sandaled feet."

—The Nemedian Chronicles.

STAN LEE PRESENTS: CONAN THE BARBARIAN™

THE SECRET OF ASHTORETH!

MAY CROM DAMN ME FOR A FOOL!

THE ACCURSED KELKANS SERVED ME DRUGGED WINE--AND I DRANK IT LIKE A SUCKLING BABE!

I DESERVE TO BE IN THIS STINKING PRISON, A THOUSAND LEAGUES FROM NOWHERE!

IF YOU DO, MY BARBARIAN, THEN TAKE HEART IN THE FACT YOU'RE NOT HERE ALONE.

WE ALL DRANK DEEP FROM THE SAME TAINTED CUP!

ROY THOMAS WRITER/EDITOR * JOHN BUSCEMA & ERNIE CHAN ILLUSTRATORS

JOHN COSTANZA letterer

FREELY ADAPTED FROM THE STORY "THE MARCHERS OF VALHALLA" by ROBERT E. HOWARD, CREATOR OF CONAN

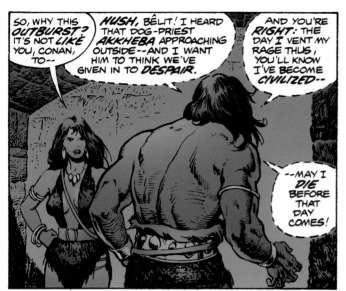

SO, WHY THIS *OUTBURST?* IT'S NOT *LIKE* YOU, CONAN, TO--

HUSH, BÊLIT! I HEARD THAT DOG-PRIEST *AKKHEBA* APPROACHING OUTSIDE--AND I WANT HIM TO THINK WE'VE GIVEN IN TO *DESPAIR.*

AND YOU'RE *RIGHT:* THE DAY I VENT MY *RAGE* THUS, YOU'LL KNOW I'VE BECOME *CIVILIZED*--

--MAY I *DIE* BEFORE THAT DAY COMES!

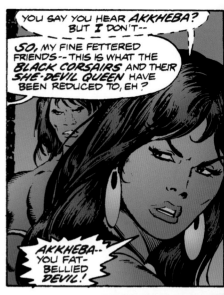

YOU SAY YOU HEAR *AKKHEBA?* BUT *I* DON'T--

SO, MY FINE FETTERED FRIENDS-- THIS IS WHAT THE *BLACK CORSAIRS* AND THEIR *SHE-DEVIL* QUEEN HAVE BEEN REDUCED TO, EH?

AKKHEBA-- YOU FAT-BELLIED *DEVIL!*

A FAT BELLY IS THE SIGN OF *PROSPERITY*-- AND THAT IS WHAT I *HAVE,* NOW THAT YOU'VE HELPED ME *SOLIDIFY* MY RULE OVER THE PEOPLE OF *KELKA.*

SINCE YOU DEFEATED THE *BARACHAN PIRATES* FOR US, THEY WILL NOT *RETURN* FOR MANY A MOON--

THUS, I COULD AFFORD TO PUT *YOU,* AS WELL AS MY *LOCAL* ENEMIES, BEHIND *BARS.*

AS A *REWARD,* I SHALL TELL MY MINIONS TO GRIND THE *RITUAL KNIFE* EXTRA SHARP, TOMORROW NIGHT--

--WHEN YOU ARE ALL *SACRIFICED* TO THE GREAT GODDESS *ASHTORETH!*

THE GROSS PRIEST'S HARSH *LAUGHTER* RESOUNDS THRU THE SUBTERRANEAN DUNGEON, SECONDS AFTER HIS *FOOT-STEPS* HAVE FADED.

THEN, IT IS SUB-CHIEF *M'GORA* WHO BREAKS THE DARK SILENCE...

GODDESS! AMRA! *

THIS *STONE* AT THE REAR OF THE CELL--IT SEEMS TO BE *LOOSE!*

BUT--IT IS STILL SO *HEAVY*-- I CANNOT *MOVE* IT--!

*BÊLIT IS CONSIDERED A *GODDESS* BY HER BLACK CORSAIRS; CONAN IS KNOWN AS *AMRA,* THE LION. --R.T.

THEN *STAND ASIDE,* MAN--BECAUSE *I CAN!* I--*MMFFF!*

LOOK, GIRL! WHILE WE PLAYED GAMES WITH *AKKHEBA, M'GORA* FOUND US AN *ESCAPE HATCH.*

WHY DO YOU THINK I MADE HIM OUR *NEXT-IN-COMMAND,* MY LOVER?

LET'S GET *OUT* OF HERE!

YET--THIS WAS SO *CONVENIENT!* DO YOU SUPPOSE--IT'S SOME SORT OF *TRAP?*

WHY WOULD AKKHEBA DO *THAT,* WHEN HE ALREADY *HAD* US?

NO, I EXPECT THE *BUILDERS* OF THE CITY PUT THIS TUNNEL HERE--

--THOSE WHO INHABITED KELKA LONG *BEFORE* THE PRESENT-DAY APELINGS!

AND HERE'S THE *PROOF* OF THE PORRIDGE!

WE'VE COME OUT ON A *CLIFF,* HIGH ABOVE THE WALLED CITY!

AND OUR *SHIP?* WHERE'S THE *TIGRESS?*

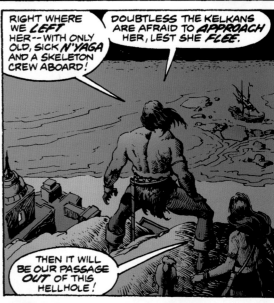

RIGHT WHERE WE *LEFT* HER--WITH ONLY OLD, SICK N'YAGA AND A SKELETON CREW ABOARD!

DOUBTLESS THE KELKANS ARE AFRAID TO *APPROACH* HER, LEST SHE *FLEE.*

THEN IT WILL BE OUR PASSAGE *OUT* OF THIS HELLHOLE!

FLEE, GODDESS? BUT THE *GOLD*--THE *JEWELS*--!

THOUGH I HATE TO ADMIT IT--FOR *ONCE,* BÊLIT, I STAND WITH *KAWAKU.*

WE *OWE* AKKHEBA SOMETHING--BESIDES, WHY LOSE THE *GOLD* WE EARNED PROTECTING THE CITY?

IT'S NOT *GOLD* YOU'RE THINKING OF--BUT THAT YELLOW-HAIRED WENCH *ALUNA!*

WHY, YOU GREEN-EYED *DEVIL-CAT!* WHEN WILL YOU EVER LEARN TO CONTROL YOUR *JEALOUSY*--AND THAT *SHEMITE TEMPER?*

AYE, I'D LIKE TO RESCUE ALUNA FROM THEIR CLUTCHES--BECAUSE SHE'S OBVIOUSLY FROM THE *MAINLAND,* AS WE ARE.

STILL, IT'S *GOLD COINS* I'M MOSTLY THINKING OF--*NOT* GOLD HAIR!

SO, I'M GOING BACK--WHATEVER YOU DECIDE FOR YOURSELF AND YOUR CORSAIRS!

YOU BATTLE-SCARRED--! YOU SAY YOU LOVE ME--YET YOU WOULD ABANDON ME THUS?

IT SERVES ME RIGHT! I SHOULD HAVE KNOWN BETTER THAN TO LOVE ONE WHO JOINED MY PIRATE BAND ONLY TO ESCAPE WALKING THE PLANK! I--

OH, SHUT UP!

THERE! IF THAT DOESN'T CONVINCE YOU I LOVE YOU--HOWEVER WE MIGHT HAVE MET--THEN HAUL OUT THE PLANK WHEN NEXT OUR PATHS CROSS!

BUT, IN THE MEANTIME, I'VE BUSINESS IN KELKA.

WELL?

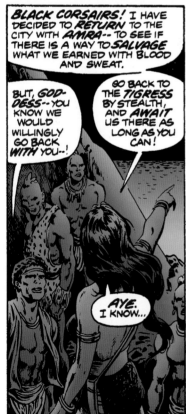

BLACK CORSAIRS! I HAVE DECIDED TO RETURN TO THE CITY WITH AMRA-- TO SEE IF THERE IS A WAY TO SALVAGE WHAT WE EARNED WITH BLOOD AND SWEAT.

BUT, GODDESS-- YOU KNOW WE WOULD WILLINGLY GO BACK WITH YOU--!

GO BACK TO THE TIGRESS BY STEALTH, AND AWAIT US THERE AS LONG AS YOU CAN!

AYE. I KNOW...

YET, THERE ARE SOME THINGS BETTER DONE BY TWO THAN BY ONE--

AND, SLINKING ABOUT KELKA IS ONLY ONE OF THEM-- EH, MY AMRA?

WHATEVER YOU SAY... GODDESS.

THEN, LET'S BE OFF--

--WHILE THERE'S STILL NOTHING MORE THAN THE PALEST OF MOONS TO BETRAY US!

KAWAKU IS NOT ONE OF THE BEST-LOVED OF THE TIGRESS' CREW, SINCE HIS RECENT DISPLAYS OF COWARDICE.

THUS, HE IS NOT MISSED AT ONCE.

AND, SOON AFTERWARD...

STEADY, BÊLIT! N'YAGA SHOULD HAVE TAUGHT YOU HILL-SCALING IN THE SOUTHERN ISLES, ALONG WITH YOUR OTHER SKILLS.

WHY-- WHEN THERE ARE ALMOST NO HILLS THERE?

BY ISHTAR, I WISH WE'D NOT SAVED THIS VILE LOST CITY!

I'D RATHER WE'D LET AURO AND HIS BARACHAN PIRATES TAKE IT!

THERE GOES YOUR TEMPER AGAIN, GIRL.

IF WE'D NOT REBUFFED THAT GOLD-BEARDED BUCCANEER--

--THERE'D BE NO LOOT LEFT IN THE CITY FOR US TO TAKE!

DROP NOW--

TRUST ME!

GOOD! BUT YOU SHOULD RELAX MORE WHEN YOU FALL.

SAVE THE LESSONS FOR LATER!

WHERE WILL WE FIND THAT BACK-STABBING PRIEST OF ASHTOR-ETH?

HARD TELLING-- SINCE THE SACRIFICE IS SCHEDULED FOR THE MORROW, HE'S LIKELY TO BE CAROUSING ANYWHERE.

NOW, SOFTLY, WOMAN--

FOR, CROM TAKE ME-- I THINK I SEE OUR STEEL DOWN BELOW!

BLAST YOU, DROMIG--I SAY THE OUTLANDER'S BROADSWORD IS THE BETTER WEAPON!

BETTER THAN OUR SPEARS, PERHAPS--

BUT, I SAY IT'S THE CUTLASS, WHICH I PERSONALLY LIFTED OFF THE DRUGGED SHE-DEVIL!

YOU ARE *BOTH* WRONG, DOGS OF KELKA!

NEITHER BLADE IS ANY GOOD-- WHEN IT IS WIELDED BY A *BLIND MAN* OR A *FOOL!*

UNNN

OOOFF

MITRA! IF *THAT'S* ALL THE OPPOSITION WE FIND, WE MAY AS WELL *TAKE OVER* THE WHOLE CITY, AND CROWN OURSELVES *KING AND QUEEN.*

NOT THE *WORST* IDEA YOU'VE EVER HAD, MY *BARBARIAN.*

WAIT! LET'S SEE WHAT'S DOING IN *HERE--!*

NO *AKKHEBA*-- BUT THE *WINE'S* FLOWING EVEN MORE FREELY THAN WHEN IT WAS *DRUGGED.*

STRANGE THAT ALL THE *WOMEN* OF THIS TIME-LOST CITY ARE SO *LOVELY*-- WHILE THE *MEN* ARE MERE *BRUTES.*

I SUSPECT THE WOMEN ARE ALL *SLAVES,* TAKEN FROM *SHIPS* WHICH STORMS HAVE TOSSED ON THE ROCKS, AS ONE DID *OURS.*

THAT IS WHY *ALUNA* WAS SUCH A RARITY SHE WAS MADE A *PRIESTESS OF ASHTORETH.*

WHERE IS GREAT *AKKHEBA,* WARTHO-- NOW THAT THE *CORSAIRS* ALL ARE IMPRISONED?

FEW *YELLOW-HAIRED FEMALES* SUCH AS SHE PROBABLY WIND UP ON THESE SHORES. I--*SHHH!*

DIDN'T YOU *HEAR?* HE IS *CELEBRATING* HIS VICTORY BY OFFERING SACRIFICE *THIS* NIGHT INSTEAD OF *TOMORROW.*

THEY SAY THE *BLOND WENCH ALUNA* IS TO BE THIS NIGHT'S OFFERING,...

...THOUGH, WE'LL *KNOW* ONLY IF WE HAPPEN TO HEAR HER *DEATH-SHRIEK,* WAFTING DOWN FROM THE *TEMPLE OF ASHTORETH.*

BÊLIT COULD *ARGUE* WITH THE *CIMMERIAN* ABOUT THEIR *NEXT* MOVE.

SHE DOES *NOT.*

THRU THE SHADOWED, GHOSTLY CITY THEY STRIDE-- WHERE THE ONLY *SOUND* IS THE STRIDENT, UNNATURAL *REVELRY* FROM THE GREAT HALL BEHIND THEM.

ONLY BEFORE THE *TEMPLE* ITSELF DO KELKANS STILL WALK *ARMED*-- AND THESE ARE HARDLY EXPECTING ANY *TROUBLE* AT THIS LATE DATE.

ALL THE *SAME*--THEY ARE ABOUT TO *GET* IT!

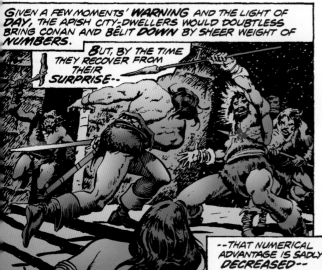

GIVEN A FEW MOMENTS' *WARNING* AND THE LIGHT OF *DAY*, THE APISH CITY-DWELLERS WOULD DOUBTLESS BRING CONAN AND BÊLIT *DOWN* BY SHEER WEIGHT OF *NUMBERS.*

BUT, BY THE *TIME* THEY RECOVER FROM THEIR *SURPRISE--*

--THAT NUMERICAL ADVANTAGE IS SADLY *DECREASED--*

--TILL IT BECOMES *NONEXISTENT--*

AND THEN, ONLY *TWO* LIVING FIGURES STAND BEFORE THE TEMPLE DOOR.

LET'S *GO,* GIRL!

IF *AKKHEBA'S* INSIDE, I WANT *FIRST CRACK* AT HIM.

NOT ON YOUR TURBULENT *LIFE,* CIMMERIAN--!

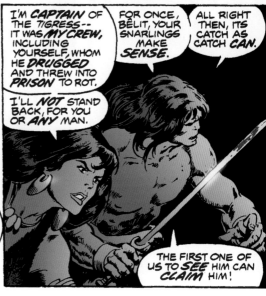

I'M *CAPTAIN* OF THE *TIGRESS*-- IT WAS *MY CREW,* INCLUDING YOURSELF, WHOM HE *DRUGGED* AND THREW INTO *PRISON* TO ROT.

I'LL *NOT* STAND BACK, FOR YOU OR *ANY* MAN.

FOR ONCE, BÊLIT, YOUR SNARLINGS MAKE *SENSE.*

ALL RIGHT THEN, ITS *CATCH* AS CATCH *CAN.*

THE FIRST ONE OF US TO *SEE* HIM CAN *CLAIM* HIM!

135

A DEEP-LYING *GLOOM* PERVADES THE TEMPLE, AS THE TWO GRIM PIRATES MOUNT THE SPIRALING STEPS. BUT, LONG BEFORE THEY CAN REACH THE SKY-REACHING *TOP*--

AAIEE

ALUNA!

AND *STILL* THE COLD STONE STAIRS STRETCH OUT *ABOVE* THEM--

--TILL, SOME SECONDS LATER, THEY BURST INTO A HIGH-DOMED, TORCH-LIT *CHAMBER*:

CROM!

EYES OF ISHTAR!

CONAN NEED NOT *ENTER* THE ROOM TO NOTE THE *NATURE* OF THE DEAD GIRL'S *SACRIFICE*.

ANOTHER *LIVING HEART* HAS BEEN SACRIFICED TO THE GRIM GODDESS CALLED *ASHTORETH*.

AND SUDDENLY, EVEN *BÉLIT* FEELS SORE *ASHAMED* FOR THE WHOLE OF HUMANKIND.

JUST THEN, A *FACE* APPEARS FROM BEHIND A TAPESTRIED DOORWAY, PRECEDED BY A FLESHY *HAND* THAT HOLDS A DRIPPING KNIFE.

EYES *WIDEN* ABRUPTLY, IN RECOGNITION AND IN *FEAR*--

YOU!

AKKHEBA!

COME *BACK* HERE, YOU MURDERING SPAWN OF *ERLIK!*

HE CAN'T GET *FAR!* WE'RE RIGHT *BEHIND* HIM.

YOU'VE FORGOTTEN YOUR *CHILDHOOD* SPENT IN THE ROYAL PALACE AS *ASGALUN*, GIRL.

THE HOMES OF *KINGS* AND *GODS* ARE AS HONEYCOMBED WITH *TUNNELS* AS THEY ARE WITH *PLOTTERS*.

DAMN HIM! WHERE'D HE GO?

MAYBE I DIDN'T *LIKE* ALUNA MUCH--BUT TO DIE *THAT* WAY--BENEATH A *BUTCHER'S BLADE*--!

THAT *DOG-PRIEST* WILL DIE A FAR *BLOODIER* DEATH, IF I--

WHAT'S THAT *SOUND?*

EH? I DON'T--

WAIT! *NOW* I HEAR IT.

THE *SOBBING* OF A WOMAN--!

IT COMES FROM UP THESE STAIRS--THE TOP OF THE TOWER WHERE ALUNA SAID *ASHTORETH* HERSELF DWELLS!

CAREFUL, MY LOVER!

I'M NOT *QUITE* AS RECKLESS AS I APPEAR--ESPECIALLY WHEN GOING TO FACE A *DEVIL-GODDESS!*

BUT, AT LEAST IT'S DOUBTFUL *AKKHEBA* PASSED THIS WAY RECENTLY.

WE'D HAVE HEARD THESE *BARS* CLANGING INTO PLACE.

WELL, I'VE BROKEN THRU-- FAR *THICKER* BARS--

UHHHH--!

--TO GET WHERE I WANTED TO *GO!*

LISTEN! THE SOBBING IS COMING FROM THAT *DOORWAY* JUST AHEAD.

IF IT'S A *TRAP*--

--THAT KELKAN DEVIL WILL WISH HE'D NEVER *SET* IT!

COME ON!

YET, NO *SCHEMER'S SNARE* AWAITS THE OUTLANDERS AS THEY RUSH LIKE WARY *WOLVES* INTO A DINGY, ILL-LIGHTED CHAMBER...

...BUT ONLY A *GIRL,* WEEPING UPON A PILE OF STRAW-- THE WEALS OF THE *LASH* VISIBLE UPON HER PALE BODY, EVEN IN THE DIMNESS.

WHERE'S THE GODDESS *ASHTORETH,* GIRL?

I AM ASHTORETH.

HER VOICE IS SOFT AS DISTANT *GOLDEN CHIMES,* THOUGH BROKEN NOW WITH *SOBBING.*

OH, *WHO-EVER* YOU ARE-- GRANT ME ONE TOUCH OF *MERCY,* IF THERE BE MERCY LEFT IN THE WORLD AT ALL!

CUT MY *HEAD* FROM MY BODY-- AND *END* THIS LONG AGONY!

YOU-- *ASHTORETH?* THAT'S *BLASPHEMY!*

I AM *SHEMITE--* AND I KNOW THAT ASHTORETH IS A *GOOD* DEITY, ALLWISE AND *LOVING.*

STOP *TREMBLING,* GIRL! WE CAME TO SLAY A *BLOODY GODDESS,* NOT A WHIMPERING *SLAVE.*

NOW, WHO *ARE* YOU-- AND NON-OF THIS NONE SENSE ABOUT *ASHTORETH!*

I AM SHE-- AND YET I AM *NOT.*

LISTEN-- THEN GRANT ME THE STROKE OF YOUR *SWORDS--!*

"ONCE I WAS *ASTARTA,* DAUGHTER OF A *KING* IN A LAND FAR TO THE *WEST* OF THIS ISLE OF KELKA."

"BY CROM, DON'T *LIE* TO US, WOMAN! THERE'S *NOTHING* WEST OF HERE-- JUST OCEAN AND *WORLD'S END!*"

"YOU ARE *WRONG--* THOUGH I WISH YOU WERE *NOT,* SINCE THEN I WOULD NEVER HAVE *LIVED!*"

"FOR, IN THAT *DISTANT PLACE,* IT WAS WORSE TO BE A *KING'S DAUGHTER* THAN THE LOW-LIEST *SLAVE!*"

"YOU SEE, AS A YOUNG GIRL, I WAS *WED*--TO A *SEA-GOD* SO ANCIENT AND AWESOME THAT MY PEOPLE HAD *FORGOTTEN* HIS VERY NAME!

"IN THE MYSTERIOUS *BRIDAL NIGHT*, WHEN I FLOATED UN-HARMED ON THE BREAST OF THE OCEAN, THE GOD *ROSE* BEFORE ME...

"AND HE GAVE TO ME THE GIFT OF *LIFE EVERLASTING*, WHICH HAS BECOME AS A *CURSE* IN THE LONG CENTURIES SINCE.

"WITH THE DAWN, I *RETURNED* TO MY PALACE HOME, WHERE I DWELT FOR YEARS, *YOUNG AND BEAUTIFUL*--

"--WHILE MY *ONCE-PLAYMATES* GREW OLD AND GREY AND *WITH-ERED* ABOUT ME.

"THEN--AT WHAT MUST BE THE SAME MOMENT THAT THE OCEANS DRANK *ATLANTIS'* GLEAMING CITIES, THE *SEA-GOD* ROSE AGAIN AND SHOOK HIS *FOAM-ING MANE*--

"--AND THE COASTAL CITIES OF *MY* LAND, TOO, WERE SWALLOWED UP BY HIS ALL-CONSUMING *ANGER* AT A LAND HALF A WORLD *AWAY!*

"YET, HE DID NOT *FORGET* ME ENTIRELY--

"BUT *LIFTED* ME GENTLY ON HIS BOSOM AND BORE ME UN-HARMED TOWARD A *DISTANT ISLAND.*

"THAT ISLE WAS *KELKA*, IN THE DAYS WHEN THE *BUILDERS* OF THIS CITY RULED IT--A *CIVILIZED* PEOPLE, WHO CLAIMED DESCENT FROM *MAINLANDERS* OF THE NOW-CHANGED *THURIAN CON-TINENT.*

"*GARBLING* MY NAME, THEY THOUGHT ME *ASHTORETH*--WHOM THEY HAD TAKEN AS THEIR *NEW GODDESS.*

"THUS, THEY FELL DOWN AND *WORSHIPPED* ME--AS IF *I* WERE SHE.

"BUT THE *HIGH PRIESTS* OF THAT PEOPLE WERE *DEVILS* THEN, JUST AS THEIR *SUCCES-SORS* ARE TODAY--AND SO, TO KEEP ME FROM BECOMING A *THREAT* TO THEIR POWER, THEY PENT ME UP *HERE.*

"FOR LONG, *UNTOLD YEARS* I HAVE BEEN WORSHIPPED--FIRST BY THE *ORIGINAL* KELKANS--THEN BY THEIR SAVAGE *HEIRS!*

"*ONE* HAS TREATED ME AS CRUELLY AS THE *OTHER* --YET ALWAYS KEPT ME IN *AWE*, BECAUSE I WAS *IMMORTAL.*

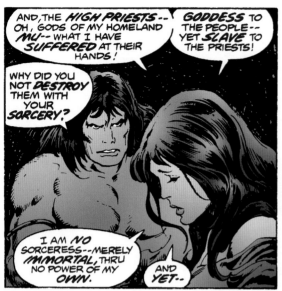

AND, THE *HIGH PRIESTS*-- OH, GODS OF MY HOMELAND *MU*-- WHAT I HAVE *SUFFERED* AT THEIR HANDS!

GODDESS TO THE PEOPLE-- YET *SLAVE* TO THE PRIESTS!

WHY DID YOU NOT *DESTROY* THEM WITH YOUR *SORCERY?*

I AM *NO SORCERESS*--MERELY *IMMORTAL*, THRU NO POWER OF MY *OWN.*

AND *YET--*

AND YET, THERE *IS* ONE SORCERY I MIGHT INVOKE-- ONE TERRIBLE, OVER- WHELMING *DOOM--*

--IF ONLY I MIGHT *ESCAPE* FROM THIS PRISON, TO STAND UP IN THE *DAWN* AND CALL UPON MY *SEA- GOD LORD!*

IN THE STILL NIGHTS, I HEAR HIM *ROARING--*

YET, THE HIGH PRIESTS' *OWN* MAGIC KEEPS HIM FROM *HEARING* MY VOICE.

AH, BUT IF THAT POWER WERE *BROKEN*--IF I COULD *LOOK* UPON THE GREAT BLUE MONSTER ONCE MORE--!

BUT, ALAS--I *CANNOT...!*

I *HOPE* NOT! STILL--WHAT'S THAT *SOUND* FROM BELOW?

LET ME *LOOK!*

TREACHERY!

THE *BARACHAN PIRATES*--THEY'RE *RETURNED,* AND GAINED ACCESS TO THE *CITY* SOME- HOW!

AND THERE'S THAT DEVIL *AURO* AT THEIR *HEAD!*

COME, BÊLIT! *WE'VE* NO PART IN THIS, SO LET'S--

DAMN!

IN, YOU APES!

IN, AT THE BIDDING OF ONE WHO HAS KEPT HIS BLOODLINE *PURE!*

SLAY THEM! SLAY *ALL* IN THE TOWER- ROOM!

"ALL!" INSTANTLY, CONAN SENSES THAT AKKHEBA MEANS THE GIRL HE KNOWS AS ASHTORETH, AS WELL.

THE MOMENT HAS COME, EVIDENTLY, FOR GODDESSES WHO KNOW TOO MUCH TO DIE--IF A SPEAR CAN KILL THEM WHERE TIME CANNOT.

CONAN WONDERS IF IT WOULD WORK.

YET, THE THOUGHT IS BUT A PASSING ONE, TO HIM AND TO BÊLIT.

FOR WITHOUT A WORD BEING SPOKEN BETWEEN THEM, THEY FIGHT AS ONE UNIT...

...TWIN HARBINGERS OF HELL, REAPING DEATH AND SLAUGHTER BOTH FOR THEIR OWN LIVES AND FOR THE LIVES OF THE AGELESS GIRL...

...AS IF TO SAVE HER LIFE WILL ATTONE FOR THE ONE WHO PERISHED SO TERRIBLY THIS NIGHT!

AKKHEBA HAS MISCALCULATED, FOR ONCE IN HIS LONG LIFE; HE BROUGHT FAR TOO FEW MEN WITH HIM TO HOPE TO OVER-WHELM TWO DEVILS WHO HOLD THE HIGH GROUND.

THUS, HE RACES ALONG ANOTHER WINDING CORRI-DOR, WITH A SPEED WHICH BELIES THE SHIMMERING BULK HE CARRIES.

BUT, THEN, FEAR IS A LIGHTENER OF FEET, IF NOT OF SOULS.

YOU'VE SLAIN THEM ALL!

LUCKILY, THEY COULD ONLY COME AT US ONE OR TWO AT A TIME.

WHERE'S AKKHEBA? MY SWORD'S STILL THIRSTY.

HE'S FLED, PLAGUE TAKE HIM!

IF HE *ELUDES* US AGAIN--!

NOT *THIS* TIME, BY MITRA!

I SEE HIM--RUNNING OUT INTO THE *OPEN!*

AND, IF THE LEGS *EXIST* WHICH CAN OUTSTRIP MINE--

--*THAT* FAT FROG DOES NOT POSSESS THEM!

NNOOO!

NO--PLEASE! HAVE *PITY* ON AN OLD MAN!

I AM A *MAN* OF THE *GODS*--!

YOU *HIDE* BEHIND THEM, MERELY--AND MAKE THEM THE *DIRTIER* FOR YOUR TOUCHING THEIR *CLOAKS.*

I'LL GIVE YOU BUT A *MOMENT* TO *PRAY* TO THEM TO RECEIVE YOUR LICE-RIDDEN *SOUL* --PROVIDED YOU *BELIEVE* IN THEM AT ALL.

THEN, I'LL--

ANOTHER *TIME,* ANOTHER *WOMAN* --CONAN WOULD ANGRILY *RESENT* ANYONE ROBBING HIM OF HIS OWN *REVENGE.*

BUT, THIS IS *BÊLIT,* QUEEN OF THE BLACK COAST...

AND SHE KNOWS NO *OTHER* WAY OF SAYING...SHE WAS *WRONG.*

SUDDENLY--

WHAT THE *DEVIL*--?

THE VERY *EARTH* SHAKES --BUT WHY *NOW?* I--

LOOK, WOMAN, LOOK *UP!*

A STRANGE, HAUNTING *CRY* RINGS ABOVE THE HELLISH *TUMULT* THAT RAGES BELOW-- OVER THE HOWLING OF BOTH *BARACHANS* AND *KELKANS.*

IT IS *ASTARTA,* CALLED *ASHTORETH* -- SCREAMING A FRENZIED INVOCATION IN AN *UNKNOWN TONGUE.*

AND, WITH HER CAPTOR *AKKHEBA* SLAIN--

--HER *SEA-GOD LORD* CAN *HEAR* HER!

THE VERY OCEAN HAS BEGUN TO *WRITHE* AND SHAKE THE EARTH, LIKE A *LIVING THING!*

AND IN THE PATH OF THE WAVES LIE THE *TOWERS OF KELKA!*

FLEE, STRANGERS!

FLEE THIS *DOOMED* CITY, THIS *DAMNED ISLE* -- IF YOU VALUE YOUR *LIVES!*

WE *SHALL!* BUT-- WHAT OF *YOU,* ASTARTA?

I HAVE LIVED *LONG* -- AND THE WORLD BEYOND HOLDS *NOTHING* FOR ME BUT *PAIN* --

YET, IN THE ARMS OF MY *LOVER,* THE *SEA* -- I SHALL FIND EITHER THE *DEATH* I SEEK--

--OR THE KIND OF *IMMORTAL BLISS* WHICH I HAVE EVER WISHED, YET *NEVER HAD!*

THEN, SHE TURNS *BACK* TOWARD THE FROTHING SEA-- AND *CRIES OUT* ONCE MORE.

HER ANSWER IS A *NEW* QUAKING, EVEN MORE FRIGHTENING THAN THE *OLD!*

AURO-- WAIT! WHERE ARE YOU--?

LET *GO* OF ME, YOU HEATHEN DEVIL!

GIVE THANKS I REALIZE YOU KNEW *NOTHING* OF THIS--

--OR ELSE I'D *RUN YOU THRU* BEFORE WE FLED BACK TO OUR SHIPS!

KAWAKU! I SHOULD HAVE KNOWN YOU'D BE MIXED UP IN ALL THIS, SOMEHOW!

IT WAS *YOU* WHO LET THE BARACHANS INTO THE CITY, WASN'T IT?

AYE, AND WHY *NOT?* I JOINED THE CORSAIRS FOR *BOOTY.*

YOU'D HAVE *FLED* THE ISLE, LEAVING IT *BEHIND.*

I GUESSED RIGHTLY THAT THE PIRATES HAD ANCHORED ON THE *FAR SIDE* OF THE ISLE -- SO I TOLD THEM OF THE ENTRANCE THRU THE *DUNGEON.*

THE PRISON WAS LEFT *UNMANNED,* WHEN THE KELKANS FOUND *US* GONE.

SO *WE* CAME THRU, TO LET IN THE *OTHER* PIRATES!

NOW *GO,* YOU WHITE DOG -- AND TAKE YOUR *SHE-WHELP* WITH YOU!

YOU'D *DIE,* FOOL, IF I *LET* YOU!

I WILL STAY *HERE* TO -- ARRRH--!

LUCKY FOR YOU, THE *TIGRESS* NEEDS *CREWMEN*--

--THOUGH, CROM KNOWS, IT *CAN'T* USE ALL THOSE POOR BERSERK *KELKANS* WHO ARE FLEEING *BEHIND* US!

THERE GO THE *BARACHANS* -- BUT THEY LOST JUST ENOUGH MEN THAT THEY'VE *LEFT* ONE OF THEIR *LONGBOATS!*

THAT'S THE FIRST *GOOD* NEWS I'VE HEARD THIS DAY...

FOR, CURSE THE GODS, I'D HATE TO HAVE TO *SWIM* IN THIS MAD SURF!

144

THEN, THE THUNDERINGS OF A *BREAKING WORLD* ARE IN THE PIRATES' EARS, AS THE ANGRY SEA *ENGULFS* THE TIME-LOST CITY AND ITS ISLAND--

--AND CONAN IS *GLAD,* EVEN AMONG THE CATACLYSM, THAT *AKKHEBA* DIED AT THEIR HAND, BEFORE A *WAVE* TOUCHED HIM!

NOR IS *EVERYONE* EQUALLY SURPRISED WHEN THE OCEAN IS ABRUPTLY *CALM* ONCE MORE.

HO, THE *TIGRESS!* WE'LL HAVE TO MEET ON THE *OPEN SEA* ONE DAY--

AND THEN WE'LL SEE HOW *BLACK CORSAIRS* FARE AGAINST *BARACHANS!*

ONE DAY-- BUT NOT *TODAY,* AURO!

NO, *NOT* TODAY-- FOR WHAT BUSINESS HAVE MERE *MORTALS* TRYING TO SETTLE THEIR PETTY SQUABBLES, WHEN *GODS* ARE ABROAD?

BUT *STILL*-- PERHAPS ONE DAY SOONER THAN YOU *THINK*--

"--AYE, PERHAPS SOONER THAN *EITHER* OF US THINKS!"

WE'LL FRET OVER THAT DAY WHEN IT *COMES.*

I KEEP WONDERING IF THE GIRL *ASTARTA* DIED, TOO-- OR IF SHE WAS *CARRIED OFF*--

--LIKE THE *BRIDE* SHE STILL WAS!

A *SILLY* CUSTOM, FOR GODS *OR* MEN-- *CARRYING OFF* A BRIDE!

WHY, I'D LIKE TO SEE *ANY*--

YOU WERE *SAYING,* GIRL?

I WAS SAYING, MY BARBAR- IAN, THAT THERE *ARE* A FEW CUSTOMS EVEN OLD *N'YAGA* NEVER TAUGHT ME...

... SO PERHAPS I *DO* HAVE A THING OR TWO TO LEARN AFTER *ALL*...!

END

145

Into The Jungle

Personal Notes on Marvel's
Conan the Barbarian #60-63, 65, 69-71
by Roy Thomas

Funny how things work out.

If you're not going to lead off a volume of this series with the story from Marvel's **Conan the Barbarian #58**, in which the Cimmerian became the "first mate" (in more ways than one) of the she-pirate Bêlit—or maybe #57, which was an expanded prequel to that story—since both those events saw print in our previous volume—then surely the next-best thing is to begin with #60, as this edition does.

For, at this point, having adapted the first part of Robert E. Howard's tale "Queen of the Black Coast" in #58 and then having opted for giving her a rousing backstory, years before Poul Anderson or anyone else did, I launched the corsair pair on their first real adventure together.

Since the *Tigress* and her crew were sailing up and down the coast of the Hyborian Age-equivalent of Africa, and mostly avoiding the Stygians (who were the Ancient Egyptians of their fictitious day), the story arc that occurred to me was, like they say, a natural.

"Conan Meets Tarzan"!

I'd been a fan of Tarzan and the other writings of Edgar Rice Burroughs since I was eight or ten and discovered that the small-town library in Jackson, Missouri, owned a semi-complete set of his works . . . at a time when, as I'd later learn, most libraries wouldn't have allowed such "trash" on their shelves . . . and the first action movie I can recall seeing, around age four or five, was **Tarzan's Desert Mystery**, with Johnny Weissmuller and a giant spider which was straight out of "The Tower of the Elephant," which would become my favorite Conan story. I was a big fan of Tarzan . . . and of his fellow comic-book Tarzan wannabes such as Kaänga and Jo-Jo the Congo King, not to mention the far-more-common white jungle goddesses like Sheena and her ilk.

In fact, the first time I recall being aware of Tarzan, not long before the Frazetta-fronted paperbacks started coming out, was Richard Lupoff's 1965 book **Edgar Rice Burroughs: Master of Adventure**, probably the first book to deal seriously with the fiction of Tarzan's creator. In a chapter on copycats of the original jungle lord, Dick said he "hesitated" to call REH's hero an "imitation of Tarzan," since, though ERB's influence on him was "great," Howard's own imagination "was so powerful that any Tarzan in Conan tends to be submerged in the latter's roaring, brawling, drinking personality." He summed up the differences and similarities: "Like Tarzan he [Conan] is periodically imprisoned, makes good his escape, defies cruel monarchs, he is a demon fighter. Unlike Tarzan, when a wench throws herself at him he is not reluctant to respond with enthusiasm."

Sounded intriguing. I'd been buying the many Burroughs-related paperbacks that were hitting the racks in the mid-1960s, both ERB himself and his various imitators—including, as it happened, the first Robert E.

Howard book I ever owned: the Ace edition of **Almuric**, which was the Texan's two-fisted answer to ERB's John Carter of Mars. I'd bought it for my collection, but hadn't yet read it. Still, this "Conan" guy sounded interesting, and—although not till around 1969-70—I eventually became a real Conan aficionado.

But every so often the thought had often come to me—what *would* happen if, in some impossible in-between world, Conan met Tarzan?

And since, as pastiche author Lin Carter once said, "One writes the books that one wants to read"—well, when I had a chance, I took it . . . and decided to create a Hyborian Age pseudo-Tarzan for the Cimmerian to battle.

I believe it was my idea that he be a redhead, because there'd been plenty of black- and blond-haired jungle men, but I didn't recall one with scarlet tresses. And, being unaware at that time of the original comic book **Ka-Zar** of the 1940s, the hero of which had been raised by lions, I decided I'd make my man "Lord of the Lions." I liked the sound of that phrase. His origin I made a reasonably close approximation of Tarzan's, since that was part of the fun, for me. I've no idea where I came up with the name Sholu, but of course a black lion was far more exotic and fantastic than a garden-variety orange one.

I suspect Amra's own monicker came hard on the heels of the lion bit. I decided he should be called "Amra"—which, in some pseudo-language invented by REH, meant "lion." It amused me to have Conan acquire that sobriquet by which he was supposedly known along the Black Coast not from the corsairs he sailed with, but would "inherit" it, in a sense, from another of that name—a villainous Tarzan type he would kill. We may have gotten a letter or two objecting to my cavalier attitude toward the title "Amra," but if so, not enough to remember after all these years. ("Amra" isn't really as much a part of the Conan mythos as many think. The word is used only in the novel **The Hour of the Dragon**, A.K.A. **Conan the Conqueror**. It is supposedly a name by which he was called when he sailed with Bêlit—yet it is never used in "Queen of the Black Coast" itself. It was essentially an early example of "retroactive continuity," REH-style.)

I had Conan do a bit of Tarzan-style animal fighting in the stories, as well—a giant killer moth, a big warthog, that kind of thing. And of course the Dragon-Riders.

I wanted these stories set in the jungles to have a feel that was more than just another copy of Tarzan's world, so I tried to add a fantasy element to them when I could. Of course, ERB was hardly a slouch at that himself, with his prehistoric beasts of Pal-U-Don and Pellucidar. The notion of men riding around on giant crocodiles stirred my imagination—and perhaps that of artist John Buscema, as well, since he visually choreographed the battle scene in **CTB #60** so stunningly. In many ways, it was a bookend with our croc-starring "Dragon from the Inland Sea" story back in issue #39 (that's **Chronicles of Conan,** Vol. 7, to you). I don't fool myself into thinking that John especially enjoyed drawing crocodiles . . . but he did what he was called upon to do, and did it beautifully, as always.

Left to my own devices, I'd have imagined that John would have liked drawing a Tarzan type, since he was a self-admitted fan of Hal Foster's work on the **Tarzan** newspaper strip in the 1930s—but for some reason he never really wanted to draw **Tarzan** (or, I presume, a Tarzan quasi-clone), even though he did so a few years later when Marvel licensed the rights to the ape-man.

No doubt John enjoyed drawing Bêlit more, since she was a curvy female . . . yet, even there, I recall his telling me once that he didn't like drawing sword-wielding ladies like Bêlit and Red Sonja nearly as much as he did the dancing girls that the pair would've scorned. Not that you could tell these personal preferences of Big John's from the art on the page, mind—he drew all types of females with basically equal excellence.

Also adding appreciably to the mix was Steve Gan, a young artist in the far-off Philippines who was working for us through Tony & Mary DeZuniga and their "studio." I felt then, and I feel now, that Steve was a better inker for **Conan** than most who tried their hand at it.

But, after this wonderful four-issue beginning to the Buscema/Gan team, it all came crashing to an end with the very next issue. I had run across a prose story by Robert E. Howard called "The Thunder Rider," one of his various tales in which a modern-day man somehow remembers, even relives, previous lives. In the original story, John Garfield, a Caucasian with a bit of "Indian" blood, relives a past incarnation as a Great Plains warrior—one of the few times a Native American was a hero and not a bloodthirsty savage in one of REH's works. He does so by undergoing a ceremony in which, in a description written in 1978 by the great fantasist Fritz Leiber, "he hangs for long hours from a tree by rawhide thongs passed through cuts under the muscles of his back, reliving a supernatural episode in his life as Iron Heart, the Comanche war-hawk of the sixteenth century." He encounters a forgotten outpost of an ancient "wizard-kingdom." The story's heroine is described by Leiber as "a fierce Pawnee warrior-maid of mixed Indian and Spanish blood, precursor of Bêlit and Valeria and other pirate-maidens in the Conan tales." We were ahead of the great Fritz Leiber on that one: John's and my adaptation of "The Thunder Rider," with Bêlit replacing the original Conchita, came out two years before he wrote his introduction for a paperback titled **Marchers of Valhalla**.

As on other occasions, for our comics adaptation I removed the incarnation angle, and made it simply an adventure that Conan and his blade-swinging lady love had while sailing the seas. But I'll admit I lust after getting a chance to adapt "The Thunder Rider" again sometime—this time, a more faithful rendering of Howard's tale, which is clearly derived from the New World myths of the Feathered Serpent—of Quetzalcoatl and Kukulcan.

But, I was talking about how the Buscema/Gan team on **Conan the Barbarian** came to an end . . . and, in so doing, to explain why it is that, in between "Fiends of the Feathered Serpent" and the preceding four-part "Lord of the Lions" saga, issue #64 of the comic was a reprint, behind a cover which showed a scene from the "Feathered Serpent" story which had been knocked back a month.

The pages of John's pencils, all written and lettered, were mailed to the Philippines, as in the several preceding months. Only, this time, they didn't seem to be coming *back*. When we inquired somewhat frantically by phone or telegram what the hell had happened, we were told that somehow inker Steve Gan had "fallen in love" with Buscema's pencils for the "Feathered Serpent" story (they *were* more than usually spectacular, I recall) and had found himself unwilling either to ink it, or to turn it back over to the DeZuniga studio. At last, we were informed, someone went and retrieved the pages from Steve—there was a hint of the threat of force in the enterprise—and the story wound up being inked by "The Tribe," which basically meant the talented Tony DeZuniga himself and whatever other inkers he could corral to help him at short notice. They did a good job . . . but I still hope that, one day before I shuffle off this mortal coil, I learn precisely what occurred halfway around the world. Not nearly all the good comic-book stories are *inside* the covers.

At this point, we—meaning Dark Horse, and I as commenter—must regrettably skip the next three issues of **Conan the Barbarian**—#66-68, to be exact—because that story arc brought Conan and Bêlit face to face with Red Sonja, the quasi-Howard heroine whose exploits are now published by a different company. Matter of fact, the last of those three issues even pulled in a time-tossed King Kull, who isn't being published by *anybody* just now. It was a rousing good multi-part yarn, and it's to be hoped that one of these days arrangements can be made for it to see publication again. But, in the meantime . . .

With issue #69, I utilized a story I'd given to a young artist named Val Mayerik. I needed to spell John B. once in a while, since he was so busy by now turning out Conan yarns both for the color comic and the black-and-white magazine **The Savage Sword of Conan**. "The Demon Out of the Deep!" was based on a decidedly minor Robert E. Howard short story set in modern times about a creature from the sea—you can pretty much figure out what the original version was by reading the Conan rendition. I didn't want to interrupt the flow of continuity when I didn't have to, so, since it was set in the Cimmerian's youth, I had him relate it to his pirate paramour on board the *Tigress*.

Next? Well, remember me mentioning a couple of paragraphs back a book called **Marchers of Valhalla**? That title came from a longish story of REH's by that name—still another of his "reincarnation" pieces, whose modern-day hero this time was a crippled and sickly Texan named John Allison. John and I turned it into yet another episode in which Conan and Bêlit land on a strange shore—and have the devil's own time ever sailing away again.

The original story had had John Allison (also the narrator of "The Garden of Fear," whose Conan adapation was reprinted in **Vol. 1** of this series) relive his life as Niord the Aesir—although his name was altered when the tale was first printed in the 1970s to Hialmar, since Niord had also been the name of another James Allison reincarnation, the hero of "The Valley of the Worm." (Is your head spinning yet? Mine is!) In Norse myth, of course, the Aesir were a race of gods; in his Conan outings Howard had turned them into a race of blond-haired Northern warriors with whom the

Cimmerian had palled around in his youth. "Marchers of Valhalla" was about an earlier eon in the life-history of such a tribe, when Niord/Hialmar wandered into a wildly prehistoric Texas—again using Fritz Leiber's words, "destroying and then perishing with a decadent kingdom of sorcerer-kings, giant serpents, and evil seductive women based on the imagined pre-Toltec Mexico and prefiguring the Stygia of the Conan tales." Thanks, Fritz—I couldn't have put it better if I'd tried for a month of Sundays, so I didn't try. In the end, the heroine of the piece turns out to be (Leiber again) "the goddess Ishtar in her various incarnations"—and she and just about everybody in sight goes down to deep-six death at tale's end.

Of course, we had to cheat. Conan and most of his crew survived the experience. Once again, though, "Marchers of Valhalla" is one of those stories that deserves to be adapted in its original form . . . and indeed, I did precisely that, some time back, with the late great Filipino artist Nestor Redondo. That version's just never been published yet, that's all . . . but hey, we only did it twenty years ago! Plenty of time yet!

It seems fitting to close this Afterword by mentioning that, with the two-part adaptation of "Marchers," we had come full circle in **Conan the Barbarian,** and Ernie Chan (then "Ernie Chua"), who had inked/embellished so many of John Buscema's stories soon after Barry Smith wandered off, was back. Ernie would stick around for a good long time, and the Buscema/Chan team would become *the* art team that many longtime readers associate with Marvel's **Conan** comic.

Also, it's with pleasure that I notice that, at the end of the final story in this volume, Conan picks up his voluptuous mate and carries her off to their cabin for fun and frolicking. A perfect note to go out on—since the next issue would begin Bêlit's quest to regain her throne in Asgalun.

Roy Thomas has been a comic-book writer and often editor since 1965 and was Marvel's editor in chief from 1972-74. In the 1970s and 1990s, he wrote the adventures of Conan the Cimmerian at various times in comic books, a newspaper comic strip, dramatic-radio-format record albums, a syndicated live-action TV series, TV animation, and in the first five drafts of the Arnold Schwarzenegger movie Conan the Destroyer. Roy currently lives with his own pirate queen, Dann, in a thirty-acre kingdom in South Carolina, where he still writes the occasional comic book, edits the monthly comics-historical magazine Alter Ego, and is at work on three books about various aspects of the history of comics.

ALSO FROM DARK HORSE

CONAN VOLUME 1 THE FROST-GIANT'S DAUGHTER AND OTHER STORIES

Collecting the first seven issues of the all-new hit series by award-winning writer Kurt Busiek (*JLA/Avengers, Astro City*) and dynamic artists Cary Nord, Thomas Yeates, and Dave Stewart. In this handsome 192-page collection, Conan wars with the murderous Vanir, meets the Frost-Giant's Daughter, and is taken as a slave by the ancient sorcerers of Hyperborea!

ISBN: 1-59307-301-1
$15.95

CONAN PVC SET THE FROST GIANT'S DAUGHTER

The Frost Giant's Daughter PVC set is the first of a series of sets of non-articulated PVC figures based on the Conan stories by Robert E. Howard. Each set features exquisitely detailed sculpting and painting. Figures designed by noted artist Arthur Suydam. Conan stands approximately 4" high; the giants are a massive 7" high.

ITEM NO.: 12-659
$44.95

CONAN THE SLAYER

Sculptor Jeffery Scott, well-known for his long tenure at Gentle Giant Studios, has captured the true essence of Conan. Exacting in its details, this piece brings forward a sculptural interpretaion of Conan that delivers the goods, and then some. 7" high, packaged in a deluxe full-color box, limited edition.

Item No.: 12-708
$49.99

CONAN LUNCH BOX

Now you may enlist the aid of Robert E. Howard's celebrated Cimmerian to help you carry your lunch. Featuring artwork by Barry Windsor-Smith, considered by many to be the ultimate Conan artist, this lunch box would serve any barbarian proudly!

ISBN: 1-59307-225-2
$14.99

AVAILABLE AT YOUR LOCAL COMICS SHOP OR BOOKSTORE
To find a comics shop in your area, call 1-888-266-4226
For more information or to order direct visit darkhorse.com or call 1-800-862-0052
Mon.-Fri. 9 A.M. to 5 P.M. Pacific Time
*Prices and availability subject to change without notice